OR

THE WACKY
BOOK OF
CHOICES
TO REVEAL
THE HIDDEN
YOU

HAT?

BY CRISPIN BOYER

**NATIONAL
GEOGRAPHIC
KiDS**

WASHINGTON, D.C.

The National Geographic Society is one of the world's
largest nonprofit scientific and educational organizations.
Founded in 1888 to "increase and diffuse geographic
knowledge," the Society's mission is to inspire people
to care about the planet. It reaches more than 400 million people
worldwide each month through its official journal, *National Geographic*,
and other magazines; National Geographic Channel; television
documentaries; music; radio; films; books; DVDs; maps; exhibitions;
live events; school publishing programs; interactive media; and
merchandise. National Geographic has funded more than 10,000
scientific research, conservation and exploration projects and
supports an education program promoting geographic literacy.

For more information, please visit nationalgeographic.com, call
1-800-NGS LINE (647-5463), or write to the following address:
National Geographic Society
1145 17th Street N.W.
Washington, D.C. 20036-4688 U.S.A.

Visit us online at nationalgeographic.com/books

For librarians and teachers: ngchildrensbooks.org

More for kids from National Geographic: kids.nationalgeographic.com

For information about special discounts for bulk purchases, please
contact National Geographic Books Special Sales: ngspecsales@ngs.org

For rights or permissions inquiries, please contact National Geographic
Books Subsidiary Rights: ngbookrights@ngs.org

Trade paperback ISBN: 978-1-4263-1557-2
Reinforced library edition ISBN: 978-1-4263-1609-8

Printed in the United States of America
14/QGT-CML/1

TABLE OF CONTENTS

DECISIONS, DECISIONS

Every hour of every day is full of decisions. Many are minor, but most add up to reveal your personality—and determine your destiny. **This** or **That?** Which will it be?

CHOOSE THIS:
Have oatmeal for breakfast.

OR

CHOOSE THAT:
Have leftover pizza for breakfast.

CHOOSE THIS:
Buy a so-so video game today.

OR

CHOOSE THAT:
Save up to get the next big system later.

CHOOSE THIS:
Pop wheelies with your buddies.

OR

CHOOSE THAT:
Pull weeds from the neighbor's yard for extra moolah.

   Welcome to the book of choices, where every answer brings you a step closer to learning something about your hidden self. Want to find out your dream career? The country that suits your idea of the good life? The species of your inner animal? Each chapter offers a series of options—some serious, some silly, some even a little sickening. Mull over the choices with your friends—or even Mom and Dad—before you choose, then turn the page to see where your decision leads.

   Don't worry about making a wrong choice—there are none. The whole point is to have fun. Besides, you've already made one smart decision: You chose to read this book!

DECISION DISSECTION!

KEEP TRACK
OF EACH TIME YOU CHOOSE

THIS!
OR
THAT!

AT THE END OF EACH CHAPTER OF *This or That?*, you'll get some professional help from Dr. Matt Bellace. He's a psychologist and stand-up comedian. Dr. Bellace will analyze your choices and determine what your decisions say about you. Through exploration and analysis of the inner workings of your mind, he'll peel you back layer by layer and you won't even realize it! But keep in mind these scenarios are just for fun. Don't like your results? Take the quiz again!

CHAPTER 1 POWER UP!

Every good superhero needs an origin story. A blast of radiation turned the Hulk mean and green. Superman crash-landed from the planet Krypton. Batman had a really rotten childhood. Your path to a career in costumed crime-fighting is much easier—you just need to pick your power! Each page in this chapter offers a choice between stupendous abilities. Will you become Captain This or the Amazing That? Soar onward and decide! But beware: With great power comes great responsibility—and sometimes there's a catch.

YOU CAN STICK TO WALLS LIKE SPIDER-MAN.

OR

CHOOSE **THAT:**

YOU CAN MOVE AT SUPERSPEED LIKE THE FLASH.

MUSE BEFORE YOU CHOOSE

Would you stick to stairs and stuff, too? Using your foot to grab the TV remote. All your photos turn out blurry. Speeding tickets for speed-walking.

9

IF YOU CHOSE **THIS**:

Peter Parker endured the bite of a radioactive spider for his amazing wall-walking abilities. Wouldn't you rather acquire yours from a cuter critter? **GECKOS** are famous for their skill at skittering up any surface—even glass. It's not gluey goop or suction cups that make these little lizards stick. Instead, their toes are coated with millions of microscopic hairs that adhere to surfaces at a molecular level, creating a bond so strong that one gecko could support 280 pounds (127 kg). Geckos lose their grip on wet surfaces, but hey—every superhero has a weakness!

IF YOU CHOSE **THAT**:

Whoosh! Whoa! Put on the breaks, buddy. Even the world's fastest animal takes time out to smell—and slurp—the flowers. **HUMMINGBIRDS** live their lives in fast-forward, with hearts that beat 1,260 times a minute as they dart from bloom to bloom sipping sugary nectar. They can zip forward, backward, up, down, and even upside down on wings that flutter 70 times per second. Scientists have declared these birds the world's fastest animals relative to their body size (only insects are faster). A dive-bombing hummingbird is speedier (relatively speaking) than the space shuttle on reentry. To feed their need for speed, the birds must eat about every ten minutes, with breaks in between to digest.

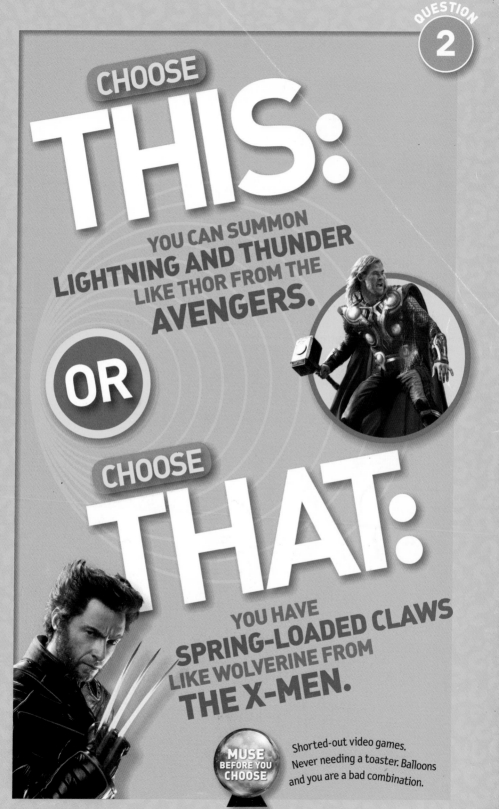

CHOOSE

THIS:

YOU CAN SUMMON
LIGHTNING AND THUNDER
LIKE THOR FROM THE
AVENGERS.

OR

CHOOSE

THAT:

YOU HAVE
SPRING-LOADED CLAWS
LIKE WOLVERINE FROM
THE X-MEN.

MUSE
BEFORE YOU
CHOOSE

Shorted-out video games.
Never needing a toaster. Balloons
and you are a bad combination.

IF YOU CHOSE THIS:

You're ready to rumble, thunder god, but don't get too proud of your loudness. The **ALPHEUS HETEROCHAELIS,** better known as the pistol shrimp, creates a much bigger bang. This small crustacean (it's littler than your little finger) wields its oversize claw just like Thor wields his hammer, unleashing an onslaught of sound and light that stuns nearby fish. By snapping its claw shut at lightning speed, the shrimp creates a tiny bubble that bursts louder than a thunderclap. Oh, and each busted bubble is accompanied by a flash of light nearly as hot as the sun's surface!

IF YOU CHOSE THAT:

Now that your arms are dangerous, you might consider keeping your claws concealed—because this power is a real pain! In the comic books, Wolverine's bionic blades slice through the skin between his knuckles (he's too much of a tough guy to say "ouch"). **CERTAIN SPECIES** of **AFRICAN FROG** know the feeling. When threatened, they pierce their skin with their own toe bones to create makeshift claws. Sometimes survival hurts!

It Could Be Worse
At least you're not a **SPANISH RIBBED NEWT.** When push comes to shove, these amphibians force their own ribs through their toxin-smeared skin to create a row of poisonous spikes.

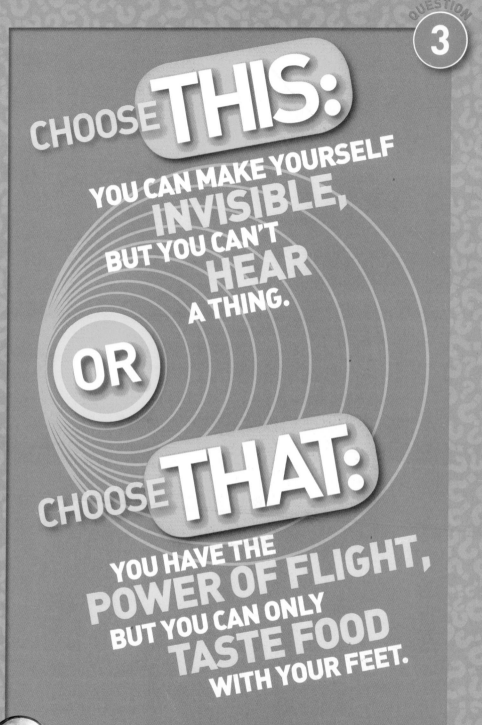

CHOOSE **THIS:**

YOU CAN MAKE YOURSELF INVISIBLE, BUT YOU CAN'T HEAR A THING.

OR

CHOOSE **THAT:**

YOU HAVE THE POWER OF FLIGHT, BUT YOU CAN ONLY TASTE FOOD WITH YOUR FEET.

MUSE BEFORE YOU CHOOSE

Never having to take the stairs.
It's not easy being sneaky when you can't hear.
Dirty sweat socks taste terrible.

IF YOU CHOSE THIS:

Then you would love life as an **OCTOPUS OR CUTTLEFISH.** Covered with tiny color-shifting skin cells called chromatophores, these cephalopods can blend in with the ocean floor to sneak up on tasty fish and evade prey. They can even change their skin texture to mimic rocks and morph into corals. Although they lack ears and are technically deaf, cephalopods can detect pressure changes in the water to sense distressed fish.

IF YOU CHOSE THAT:

Zap! You've just morphed into a **COMMON HOUSEFLY.** This winged insect buzzes through the air at five miles an hour (8 km/h) and tastes its food with hairlike receptors on its feet. Instead of a sweet tooth, you have a sweet toe! Oh, and you also spit on your food before eating it. Good luck getting invited back to the barbecue!

Dirt for dinner: At least you're not an earthworm! It has taste buds along its entire body to sample yummy soil.

CHOOSE THIS:
YOU CAN FALL ASLEEP ON COMMAND.

OR

CHOOSE THAT:
YOU NEVER NEED TO SLEEP AT ALL.

MUSE BEFORE YOU CHOOSE

Dull road trips pass in the blink of an eye. Unlimited daydreams. Bye-bye, bedtime. No more nightmares.

IF YOU CHOSE THIS:

Zzzzzz ... Bzzzt! Nap time's over! Sorry for the rude awakening, but the ability to fall asleep on command is nothing more than a pipe dream. (Falling under the spell of hypnosis doesn't count, either—it's a different mental state from sleep.) Unless you suffer from **NARCOLEPSY**— a medical condition that causes uncontrolled "sleep attacks" day or night—you'll just have to drift off to dreamland like everyone else. Or maybe you'd rather be a koala. These sleepy tree-dwelling marsupials snooze 20 hours a day (but imagine how worn out you'd be if all you ate were leaves and you had to climb to every room in your house).

IF YOU CHOSE THAT:

Humans spend about a third of their lives snoozing, which means you'll waste roughly 26 years sawing logs (based on average life expectancy in the United States). Think of all the things you'd accomplish—books written, languages learned, video games beaten—if you could do away with that down-time! Still, doctors believe that a good night's sleep comes with many benefits, including improved creativity and mental sharpness. Perhaps you could compromise and siesta like a **GIRAFFE**—an animal that dozes less than two hours a day.

Wide Awake...
Dolphins and whales sleep with their brains half awake and one eye open. New-borns don't even sleep at all for the first month.

DO NOT DISTURB

QUESTION 5

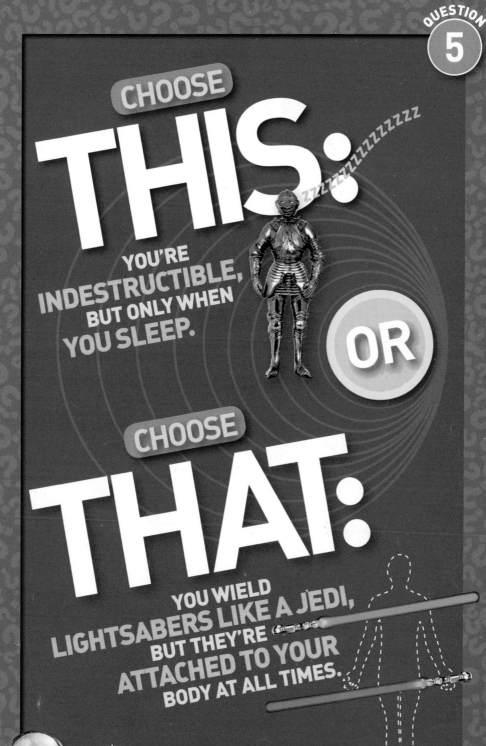

CHOOSE

THIS:

ZZZZZZZZZZZZZZZZZ

YOU'RE INDESTRUCTIBLE, BUT ONLY WHEN YOU SLEEP.

OR

CHOOSE

THAT:

YOU WIELD LIGHTSABERS LIKE A JEDI, BUT THEY'RE ATTACHED TO YOUR BODY AT ALL TIMES.

MUSE BEFORE YOU CHOOSE

Snoozing on a bed of nails. Sleep-skiing. Clothing covered in lightsaber burns.

IF YOU CHOSE THIS:

Then you're totally twinsies with a **TARDIGRADE!** Studied for their toughness, these eight-legged animals have been subjected to the most extreme conditions imaginable—including the vacuum of space! They ride out droughts and deep freezes by shutting down their bodies and rolling into balls that look like boogers. While in this switched-off state, a tardigrade is virtually indestructible. Found in soggy environments—perhaps even your own backyard—this extreme survivor would make the perfect creature in a horror flick if not for one fact: A tardigrade is a smidge smaller than the period at the end of this sentence.

IF YOU CHOSE THAT:

Now you know what life's like as a **VELVET BELLY LANTERN SHARK.** This two-foot (60-cm) fish lives in the dim, dangerous depths of the Mediterranean Sea and the Atlantic Ocean. Many deep-sea creatures glow in the dark (a phenomenon known as bioluminescence) to attract prey or blend in with the faint light from above to hide from predators. But when the lantern shark shines, it's showing off its weaponry! Dangerous spines on its two dorsal fins light up like lightsabers, letting any predators nearby know that this fish is armed and dangerous.

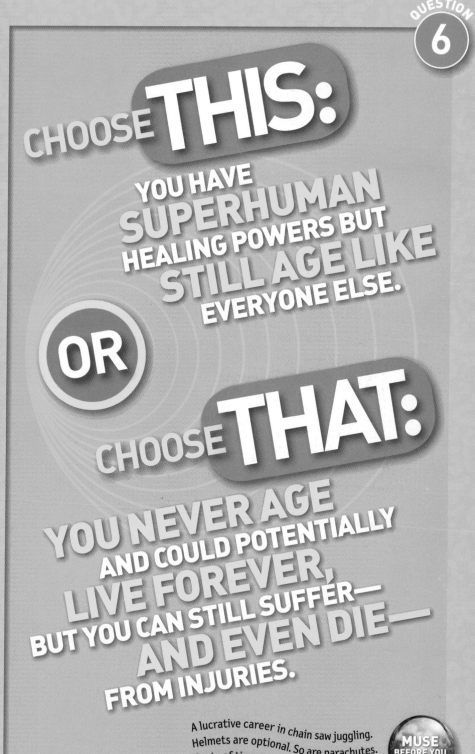

CHOOSE **THIS:**

YOU HAVE
SUPERHUMAN
HEALING POWERS BUT
STILL AGE LIKE
EVERYONE ELSE.

OR

CHOOSE **THAT:**

YOU NEVER AGE
AND COULD POTENTIALLY
LIVE FOREVER,
BUT YOU CAN STILL SUFFER—
AND EVEN DIE—
FROM INJURIES.

A lucrative career in chain saw juggling.
Helmets are optional. So are parachutes.
Plenty of time to get chores done. Fear of
injury might scare you indoors for centuries.

MUSE
BEFORE YOU
CHOOSE

IF YOU CHOSE THIS:

Run with scissors! Zoom down triple-black-diamond courses on one ski! You now have the stunning regenerative powers of an **AXOLOTL,** a friendly faced salamander that lurks in lakes near Mexico City. Lopped-off leg? Walk it off! The axolotl sprouts another in a matter of months. Broken heart? Damaged brain? No worries! They'll grow back good as new. Despite their healing abilities, axolotls are in danger of extinction from pollution and larger fish that swallow these salamanders whole. So let that be a lesson for you: You can't heal your body if there's no body left to heal.

IF YOU CHOSE THAT:

Ah, to be forever young—just like the *Turritopsis nutricula*, aka the **IMMORTAL JELLYFISH.** Although it's not really a jellyfish (technically, it's a hydrozoan), this bell-shaped ball of jelly really is capable of living forever. When the going gets tough, the creature reverts to its earliest stage of development and begins the aging process from scratch, hitting the reset button on its life. That would be like you transforming into a baby whenever you wanted! But good luck out there, kid. As any wise young *Turritopsis nutricula* will tell you, it's still a dangerous world!

CHOOSE

THIS:

YOU POSSESS THE
BRUTE STRENGTH
OF A
BEAST.

OR

CHOOSE

THAT:

YOU POSSESS THE
PROPORTIONAL
STRENGTH OF
A BUG.

MUSE
BEFORE YOU
CHOOSE

Always having to carry the groceries. Towing the car will
save Mom gas. Beastman is a better superhero name
than Bugman. But what if the bug's actually stronger?

IF YOU CHOSE THIS:

Hit the showers, muscleheads—you've got nothing on a determined **GRIZZLY BEAR** when it flexes its muscles. A 1,000-pound (453-kg) bear can toss a 700-pound (317-kg) garbage bin like a beach ball! Researchers estimate that a grizzly possesses the strength of five humans—even more if the bear gets angry. The lesson here: Never upset a grizzly!

IF YOU CHOSE THAT:

Depending on which insect you pick, you may have matched the might of the world's strongest animal (proportionally speaking, anyway). The **ONTHOPHAGUS TAURUS** dung beetle can pull more than 1,100 times its own body weight. That would be like you towing six fully loaded double-decker buses! These brutish bugs require superhero strength to battle other beetles for mates and roll their big balls of doo-doo, which serve as both dinner and nurseries for baby beetles.

Superstrength!
Astronauts and soldiers of the future will feel like superheroes when they strap on "exosuits," strength-boosting robotic outfits being developed by the military and NASA.

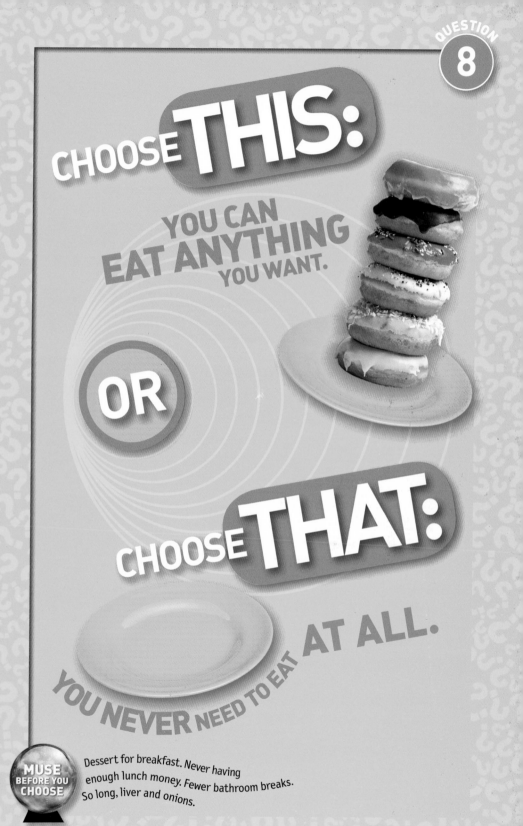

CHOOSE **THIS:**

YOU CAN
EAT ANYTHING
YOU WANT.

OR

CHOOSE **THAT:**

YOU NEVER NEED TO EAT AT ALL.

MUSE
BEFORE YOU
CHOOSE

Dessert for breakfast. Never having enough lunch money. Fewer bathroom breaks. So long, liver and onions.

IF YOU CHOSE **THIS**:

By anything, we mean *anything!* You now have the bottomless appetite of a **BULLFROG,** and nothing is off the menu. Today's all-you-can-eat buffet includes wriggling scorpions, slithering snakes, fluttering birds, furry spiders, scurrying rats, flopping fish, and squirming worms. A bullfrog will devour whatever it can pummel with its titanic tongue and cram into its massive mouth. What, did you think you'd be gobbling down ice cream and cheeseburgers? Unfortunately, such treats don't last long in a bullfrog's swampy home.

IF YOU CHOSE **THAT**:

You might be through with chewing, but you still need nourishment or you'll wither away. The **VAMPIRE BAT** has your answer: an all-liquid diet! This creepy creature of the night soars through the jungles of Central and South America looking for dinner donors—any pig, chicken, or cow will do. Once it spies a snoozing victim, the bat swoops in silently and opens a tiny cut with its razor-sharp fangs to get the blood flowing. Then, bottoms up! Between sunrise and sunset, a typical bat might consume half its weight in blood. Are you missing solid food yet?

Junk Food Diet...
Researchers predicted that in the next 30 to 50 years you'll be able to pig out to your heart's content, then swallow a "nutribot" pill filled with microscopic robots that zap the junk in your junk food.

DID YOU **KEEP TRACK** OF EACH **THIS** AND **THAT**? TURN THE PAGE TO SEE WHAT YOUR CHOICES **SAY ABOUT YOU!**

SEE WHAT YOUR CHOICES SAY ABOUT YOU.

DOC TALK...

PSYCHOLOGIST
DR. MATT BELLACE
DISSECTS YOUR
DECISIONS...

ANALYZE THIS!

CHOOSE THIS, If you mostly picked you're a practical do-it-yourself type who gets things done. You've got incredible strength and will stick around when the going gets tough. Your personality isn't flashy, but you shine (sometimes literally) when challenged. You're a flexible person who can adapt to every situation, which is great because you're going to live a thousand years. Who knows what Earth will look like then?

ANALYZE THAT!

CHOOSE THAT, If you mostly picked you love living life to extremes and getting attention. That's not necessarily a bad thing, but some extreme behavior comes at a price. It feels great to see yourself in the spotlight for accomplishing great deeds, but your flashy antics are bound to come under some negative scrutiny. If you really crave immortality, work hard toward accomplishing positive things and your legend may live on forever. Otherwise, you could earn a reputation for all the wrong reasons, which will make living forever feel like, well, forever.

CHAPTER 2
GOOD TO GO

The local zoo? Been there. Disney World? Explored that. You're ready to chart new territory, and this chapter will lead the way! Discover countries that deliver the good life, see sights that are out-of-sight, and explore oddball destinations you never knew you wanted to visit. So pack your bags and make your picks—this chapter's pages will take you places!

CHOOSE **THIS:**

WITNESS THE WORLD'S GREATEST LIGHT SHOW IN THE SKY.

OR

CHOOSE **THAT:**

CREATE YOUR OWN LIGHT SHOW IN THE SEA.

Firework finales will seem boring by comparison. Neck strain from staring up. Wrinkled fingers from playing in the water.

MUSE BEFORE YOU CHOOSE

IF YOU CHOSE **THIS**:

Bundle up and step outside to watch an **AURORA** swirl in the night sky from horizon to horizon. Ancient people believed these curtains of colored light were the spirits of ancestors dancing through the heavens, but their actual cause is no less astonishing. Auroras arise when charged particles cast off from the sun hit Earth's magnetic field 100 miles (160 km) up and make the air molecules glow green, violet, blue, or red. The result is a light show that's

literally out of this world. The best spots to see the aurora borealis (or northern lights) are Alaska, the northwestern regions of Canada, the southern tips of Iceland and Greenland, Norway, and Siberia. The aurora australis of the Southern Hemisphere is trickier to see unless you live in Antarctica.

IF YOU CHOSE **THAT**:

Kayak across the Laguna Grande, a bay on the northeastern corner of Puerto Rico, on a moonless night and you'll spot something astounding: The water glows like a night-light with each push of your paddle. Welcome to **BIOLUMINESCENT BAY,** one of the

best spots in the world to witness the phenomenon of bioluminescence. The bay is home to billions of microscopic creatures called *Pyrodinium bahamense* that shine when disturbed. Every splash makes the water flash, and darting fish create lightning bolts in the deep. Wriggle your fingers in the water and you'll feel like Harry Potter casting the *Lumos* light spell.

CHOOSE

THIS:

PLAY BASKETBALL IN THE TREETOPS.

OR

CHOOSE

THAT:

GO BOWLING UNDERGROUND.

Tricky three-pointers. Out-of-bounds is a long way down. Could a gutterball cause a cave-in?

MUSE
BEFORE YOU
CHOOSE

IF YOU CHOSE **THIS**:

Better ask Horace Burgess for directions to the basketball court when you tour the tree house he built in Crossville, Tennessee, U.S.A. Actually, it's more like a tree mansion. Cradled in the branches of a massive white oak and 6 other trees, the Minister's Treehouse has 80 rooms spread throughout 10 floors that rise 97 feet into the sky. Burgess, an ordained minister, began building the house in 1993 as an act of his godly devotion. Nearly 260,000 nails later, his creation towers above the trees' tallest branches and is still under construction. You'll find the basketball court on the third floor, in a cavernous room that doubles as a church sanctuary complete with a stained-glass window.

IF YOU CHOSE **THAT**:

Start planning your campaign for President of the United States, or at least make friends with someone in the White House. One perk of the presidency is 24-hour access to not one but two basement bowling alleys, a single lane beneath the North Portico and a double-lane alley under a building beside the West Wing. Both alleys feature automatic ball returns, electronic scorekeepers, racks of balls, and loaner shoes for guests of the President and White House staff. Make sure to bring clean socks. No need to stink up the federal footwear!

Sleep in the Trees...

If you want a little more luxury from your treetop stop, check into the Treehotel in Harads, Sweden. Each room is suspended in towering pines and offers funky design features, such as mirrored walls that blend in with the forest. One room is even shaped like a flying saucer!

CHOOSE **THIS:**

LIVE IN A PLACE WHERE THE SUN NEVER SETS.

OR

CHOOSE **THAT:**

MOVE TO A PLACE WHERE THE SUN NEVER RISES.

Saving a fortune on lightbulbs.
Befuddling bedtimes. Are you afraid
of the dark? Sayonara, sunscreen.

MUSE
BEFORE YOU
CHOOSE

IF YOU CHOSE **THIS:**

Grab your sunglasses (and your parka) and head north—far, far north—until you cross the **ARCTIC CIRCLE.** Reach this region at the top of the world and you're guaranteed at least one 24-hour period in which the sun never slips below the horizon. Known as "midnight sun," this sunshine surplus occurs on the summer solstice (June 21) and grows longer as you head farther north. The North Pole, for instance, gets six months of daylight!

IF YOU CHOSE **THAT:**

Grab your parka and head north—far, far north—until you cross the **ARCTIC CIRCLE.** Wait, isn't that the same place we sent you above for a dose of extra daylight? Well, the Arctic Circle's midnight-sun phenomenon works in reverse during the winter months. You'll experience at least one 24-hour period in which the sun never rises—on the winter solstice (December 21)—and this "polar night" grows longer as you head farther north. Why all the crazy days and nights up north? Earth is actually tilted on its axis, which exposes more or less of our planet's Northern and Southern Hemispheres to the sun depending on the time of year.

Cold Company...

You can experience the same cycle of endless days and nights at the bottom of the world in the **ANTARCTIC CIRCLE,** but that region's lack of human settlements means you'll be spending a lot of time alone and out in the cold. You're better off sticking to the Arctic Circle, which is crossed by Canada, Sweden, Russia, the U.S. state of Alaska, and several other countries with cozy accommodations.

ANTARCTIC CIRCLE

CHOOSE
THIS:
TAKE A VACATION ON THE OCEAN FLOOR.

OR

CHOOSE
THAT:
JOIN AN EXPEDITION TO MARS.

MUSE
BEFORE YOU
CHOOSE

Peeping tunas. Claustrophobic quarters. Hopping home in low gravity. Bidding your Earthling friends a teary farewell.

IF YOU CHOSE THIS:

Why not sleep with the fishes in style? The **ATLANTIS,** a hotel in the Middle Eastern nation of the United Arab Emirates, offers posh aquatic accommodations. Both the Neptune and Poseidon Suites (named, appropriately enough, for ancient water gods) feature floor-to-ceiling windows with underwater views of a lagoon teeming with sharks, manta rays, and thousands of other fishy friends. You're guaranteed a deep sleep!

IF YOU CHOSE THAT:

Then **MARS ONE** wants you! This Dutch project plans to send Earthlings to the red planet beginning in 2023. You don't need military training or a science degree to apply. Mars One is looking for 24 to 40 brainy adventurers who are creative, curious, and adaptable. Make the cut and you'll undergo seven years of astronaut training and simulated Martian living before finally blasting off for the seven-month transit to the red planet. Oh, and before you sign on the dotted line, keep this in mind: The trip to Mars is a one-way ticket. You'll become a permanent Martian!

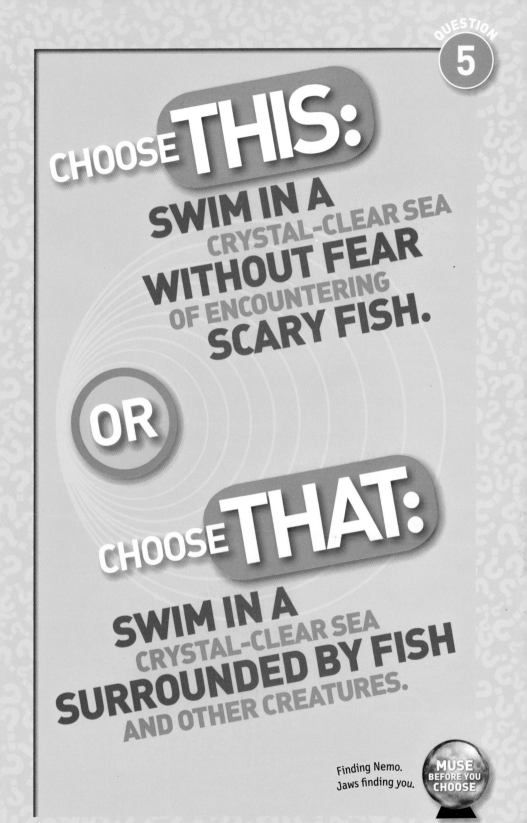

CHOOSE **THIS:**

SWIM IN A
CRYSTAL-CLEAR SEA
WITHOUT FEAR
OF ENCOUNTERING
SCARY FISH.

OR

CHOOSE **THAT:**

SWIM IN A
CRYSTAL-CLEAR SEA
SURROUNDED BY FISH
AND OTHER CREATURES.

Finding Nemo.
Jaws finding you.

MUSE
BEFORE YOU
CHOOSE

37

IF YOU CHOSE THIS: If you're skittish about swimming in the ocean, why not plunge into the world's largest swimming pool instead? Stretching more than half a mile (1 km) along the beach of Chile's **SAN ALFONSO DEL MAR RESORT** and reaching depths of 115 feet (35 m), this man-made lagoon is so massive that guests use kayaks and sailboats as pool toys. The turquoise water—all 66 million gallons (250 million L) of it—is pumped in from the Pacific and heated to 79°F (26°C). You'll feel like you're floating in the Caribbean without risking any encounters with curious sharks and roving stingrays.

IF YOU CHOSE THAT: Set sail for either the **GREAT BARRIER REEF** off the eastern coast of Australia or the **MESOAMERICAN BARRIER REEF** stretching from Mexico's Yucatán coast down to Honduras. Often called the "rain forests of the sea," coral reefs account for 25 percent of all life in the ocean. They're like living undersea cities for small fishes, shrimps, and clams—which attract larger predators such as sharks, dolphins, and sea turtles. The workers constructing these cities are the corals themselves. These minuscule creatures create a tough limestone skeleton, then invite in colorful algae roommates that convert sunlight to food and oxygen for the corals. The structures you see are the skeletons of thousands of coral polyps piled up over the centuries, so take care not to hit the reef with your flippers when you swim by. One clumsy kick can destroy decades of coral growth!

Swimming in Salt...
If you're afraid of fish *and* hate having to tread water, consider a soak in the **DEAD SEA** between Jordan and Israel. Bathers bob in the extra-salty water (ten times saltier than seawater), which is inhospitable to sea life.

Salt

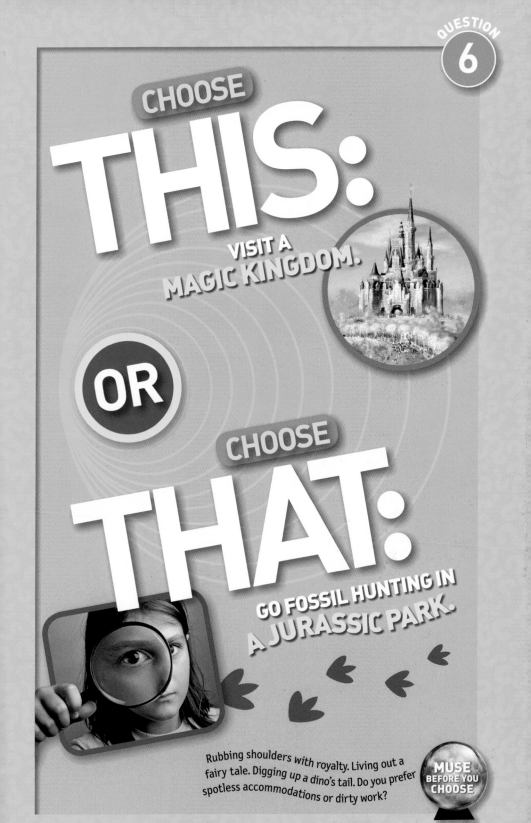

CHOOSE

THIS:

VISIT A MAGIC KINGDOM.

OR

CHOOSE

THAT:

GO FOSSIL HUNTING IN A JURASSIC PARK.

Rubbing shoulders with royalty. Living out a fairy tale. Digging up a dino's tail. Do you prefer spotless accommodations or dirty work?

MUSE BEFORE YOU CHOOSE

IF YOU CHOSE THIS:

Why settle for Disneyland's phony fortification when you can tour the palace that inspired it? On a hilltop overlooking a picturesque German village sits **NEUSCHWANSTEIN CASTLE.** This sprawling palace was built in the 19th century as a romantic, fantasy-themed reminder of the might and majesty of medieval castles. The iconic Sleeping Beauty Castle at California's Disneyland theme park was modeled after Neuschwanstein and incorporated many of its fairy-tale touches.

IF YOU CHOSE THAT:

Dinosaurs may be long gone, but they've left a trail of fossils for you to follow at the **DINOSAUR NATIONAL MONUMENT** on the U.S.'s Utah-Colorado border. Here you can hike the Fossil Discovery Trail alongside an exposed portion of the Morrison formation, a slab of sediment that formed during the late Jurassic period around 150 million years ago. It's a gold mine of dinosaur bones.

DINOSAUR
NATIONAL MONUMENT
CANYON AREA

Cozy Castle...
Can't make the trip to Germany? You can also find a magical palace at California's Hearst Castle, built for American multimillionaire William Randolph Hearst in the 1920s. Despite modern touches such as swimming pools and a movie theater, much of this mansion's design was inspired by romantic castle architecture.

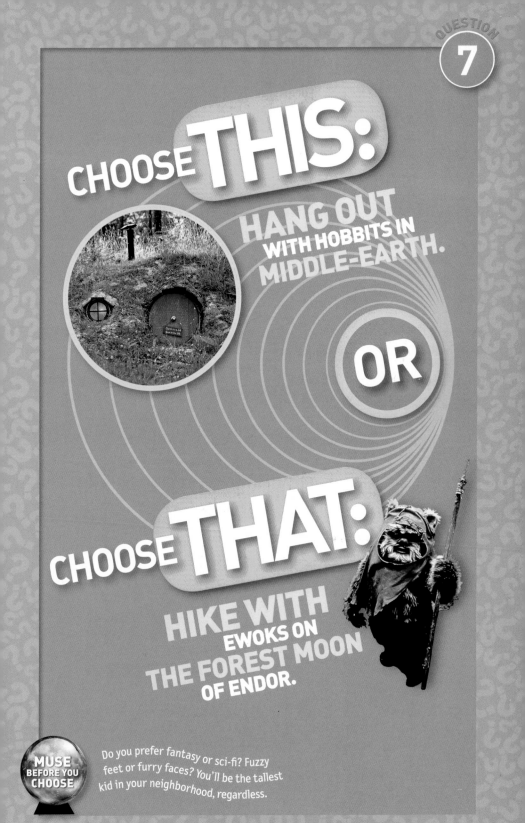

CHOOSE **THIS:**

HANG OUT WITH HOBBITS IN MIDDLE-EARTH.

OR

CHOOSE **THAT:**

HIKE WITH EWOKS ON THE FOREST MOON OF ENDOR.

MUSE BEFORE YOU CHOOSE

Do you prefer fantasy or sci-fi? Fuzzy feet or furry faces? You'll be the tallest kid in your neighborhood, regardless.

IF YOU CHOSE THIS: Turns out that Middle-earth—the make-believe realm of furry-footed hobbits—really exists on planet Earth. Director Peter Jackson filmed his Lord of the Rings and Hobbit movies in New Zealand, an island nation east of Australia. The country's wild and wildly varied terrain made the perfect match for the misty mountains and fantastical forests depicted in author J. R. R. Tolkien's fantasy novels. Visitors to the Waikato region on the North Island can even stroll through the hobbit village from the films, complete with 44 hobbit holes. You won't find any real-life hobbits (or elves or dwarves), but at least you won't run into any unsightly orcs, either!

IF YOU CHOSE THAT: Sure, you could *yub-yub* it up with actors dressed in ewok costumes at Disney's Hollywood Studios in Florida, U.S.A., but wouldn't you rather take a hike on the little furballs' home world? Their forest moon of Endor (seen in *Return of the Jedi*) was filmed in one of the Redwood National and State Parks near San Francisco, California. Home to the tallest living trees in the world—including an 800-year-old redwood titan that would tower six stories above the Statue of Liberty—these parks provide a magnificent and decidedly Endorian backdrop for your hike. You won't find any ewoks here, but perhaps you'll spot a different species of hairy beast. This is Bigfoot country!

Hobbit Humans?

If you really wanted to visit a community of hobbit-like creatures, you'd need a time machine. Scientists discovered the remains of tiny humans in caves on the Indonesian island of Flores, where these little people lived alongside pygmy elephants and komodo dragons until as recently as 13,000 years ago. Members of this species—new to science—didn't grow much taller than a modern three-year-old child. Scientists named them *Homo floresiensis*, although workers on the dig site dubbed them hobbits because of their itty-bitty stature.

DID YOU **KEEP TRACK** OF EACH THIS AND THAT ?

TURN THE PAGE TO SEE WHAT YOUR CHOICES

SAY ABOUT YOU!

DOC TALK...

PSYCHOLOGIST DR. MATT BELLACE DISSECTS YOUR DECISIONS...

ANALYZE THIS!

CHOOSE THIS, then congratulations are in order! You're one of the rare people who knows your limitations. You're willing to travel and see new things—as long as you don't have to deal with any scary surprises. You'd probably rather watch TV shows about the great outdoors than actually trek into the wilderness yourself. The upshot is you'll probably live longer (and with fewer bumps and bruises) thanks to your sense of caution. However, it's important to remember that some of the most important choices in life may require you to step outside of your comfort zone.

ANALYZE THAT!

If you mostly picked **CHOOSE THAT,** you like to see for yourself how things work. You probably watch shows in which the hosts make and destroy stuff just so you can learn how to make and destroy stuff, too. You're empowered to change the world around you, which means you'll never get stuck for long on any one problem. The bottom line is you're bright and enjoy learning, especially when it requires you to get your hands dirty. People with your personality type tend to live for excitement, but sometimes that excitement comes with discomfort and dirty fingernails.

CHAPTER 3

HELP WANTED

It's a simple question with a difficult answer: What do you want to be when you grow up? Choosing poorly might lead to disaster: years spent preparing for a daily grind at a job you dread. Hey, no pressure or anything! This chapter's choices offer a little career counseling. The options here aren't always clear—some are downright mysterious—but mull over each one carefully before turning the page. You might just land on your dream job without even realizing how you got there!

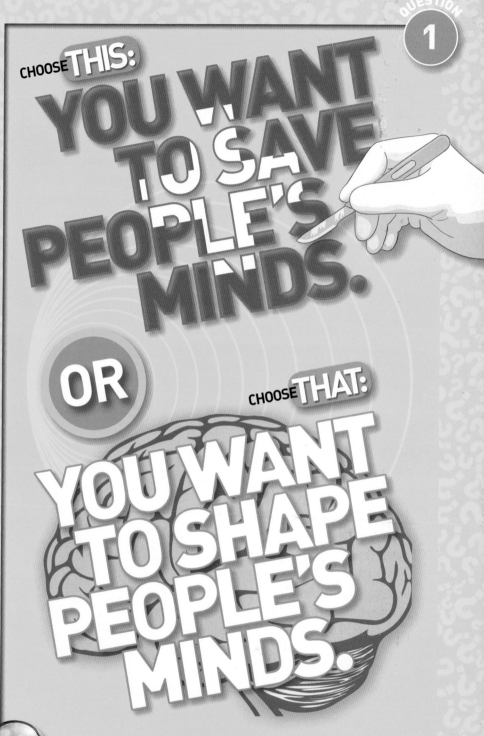

CHOOSE **THIS:**

YOU WANT TO SAVE PEOPLE'S MINDS.

OR

CHOOSE **THAT:**

YOU WANT TO SHAPE PEOPLE'S MINDS.

MUSE BEFORE YOU CHOOSE

Prolonging lives. Inspiring others to do great things.
Looming large in people's lives, regardless of your choice.

IF YOU CHOSE **THIS:**

No one saves more brains than a **NEUROSURGEON.** These highly specialized doctors remove tumors and repair gray matter damaged by accidents or disease. But the road to this prestigious career is a long one. It takes an average of 15 years of education and training after high school to become a neurosurgeon. But it's never too early to start studying hard, particularly in science class. "Medical school itself is very competitive," says Robert Louis, M.D., a brain surgeon in the University of Virginia Health System, "and only the top one percent of medical school graduates are considered for neurosurgery." The job itself takes attention to detail, steady hands, and a tolerance for working long hours with little sleep. More than anything, you need a desire to help people. "It is the motivation to heal that gets you through the long years of training and hours of work," says Dr. Louis.

IF YOU CHOSE **THAT:**

Then you should become a **TEACHER!** After all, think of all the educators who filled your noggin with bright ideas. Sure, you'll spend most of your time stuck in a classroom, but the job is rarely boring. "Each day is like a new adventure," says Deborah Glynn, who has taught elementary and middle school students for more than 30 years. "One minute you're a speaker expounding knowledge, the next you're an observer watching discoveries, and sometimes you're like a detective looking for clues." Teaching requires a college degree and credentials in multiple subjects (for teaching elementary schools) or a single subject (for high schools). Good teachers work well with others and have a passion for what they teach. "You also need to be compassionate, a good listener, and patient," Glynn says.

CHOOSE THIS:

YOU LIKE TAKING GADGETS APART AND PUTTING THEM BACK TOGETHER.

OR

CHOOSE THAT:

YOU LIKE TAKING THINGS APART, BUT YOU COULD CARE LESS ABOUT PUTTING THEM BACK TOGETHER.

MUSE BEFORE YOU CHOOSE

Getting to see how gizmos work. Mom and Dad getting mad when you break the DVD player. Demolishing things can be fun. Demolishing things can also be dangerous.

IF YOU CHOSE THIS:

Maybe you're a born **INVENTOR.** "The ability to come up with solutions to problems others don't even know exist is built into the genes," says Ralph Baer, who's known as the "father of video games" for inventing the first gaming system and light gun. (Love playing the Wii? Thank this guy!) Baer earned a college degree in engineering, but he says born inventors start learning much earlier in life, taking apart clocks, toys, and other gadgets to see how they work. The job comes with many obstacles—from filing patents to finding funding for projects—but the greatest challenge lies in maintaining an intense focus on a single invention. "You need to really love to work on one thing intensively," Baer says.

IF YOU CHOSE THAT:

Then make it your mission to get into **EXPLOSIVE DEMOLITION.** People in this field start their workday with a bang, bringing down decrepit buildings with explosives. They stick parcels of dynamite in all the right places to make each project implode—or collapse on itself—rather than blow sky-high and damage neighboring structures. Breaking into this business is tricky. Classes in physics and engineering offer some instruction in destruction, but you'll need to start on the ground floor of a demolition company and learn the job as you go. Applicants with unsteady hands need not apply.

CHOOSE
THIS:

YOU'D LIKE TO WORK WITH LIONS, TIGERS, AND BEARS.

OR

CHOOSE
THAT.

YOU'D RATHER WORK WITH SHARKS, SEALS, AND DOLPHINS.

Petting the world's largest kitty.
Ending up as big-cat chow. Dolphins are
adorable. Sharks? Not so much.

MUSE BEFORE YOU CHOOSE

IF YOU CHOSE THIS:

Welcome to the wild life of a **WILDLIFE VETERINARIAN.** Although these daring animal docs could diagnose your sick dog or cat, they specialize in treating creatures that live in the great outdoors, often helping researchers study endangered animals. Wildlife veterinarian Winston Vickers has a patient list that could populate a zoo, including foxes, mountain lions, coyotes, owls, eagles, snakes, lizards, and tortoises. Vickers says his job is all about juggling a variety of activities, from capturing animals in the wild to analyzing samples in the lab. The job requires a four-year college degree, a veterinary degree, then postgraduate work in disease studies, ecology, or a related field (typically, 10 to 13 years of school in all).

IF YOU CHOSE THAT:

Dive into a career as a **MARINE BIOLOGIST,** a scientist who studies life in the ocean. You'll have your work cut out for you— marine biologists know more about the surface of the moon than about the depths of the sea. Like any budding scientist, you'll need to study math, biology, chemistry, and even physics and statistics. But the bright side to all that bookwork is you'll polish your exploration skills, too. "Spend some time at the seashore and out on the water," says marine biologist Dr. Rod Hobbs. "Learn the practical skills of swimming, fishing, boating, and diving so that you have a personal understanding of the marine environment."

Harrowing House Calls...
Don't bother considering either of these careers unless you love the outdoors. "It can be cold and wet, strenuous, and at times a tad dangerous," says Vickers. "But the job is definitely fun and never boring—at least if you like being out in wild areas where our 'patients' live."

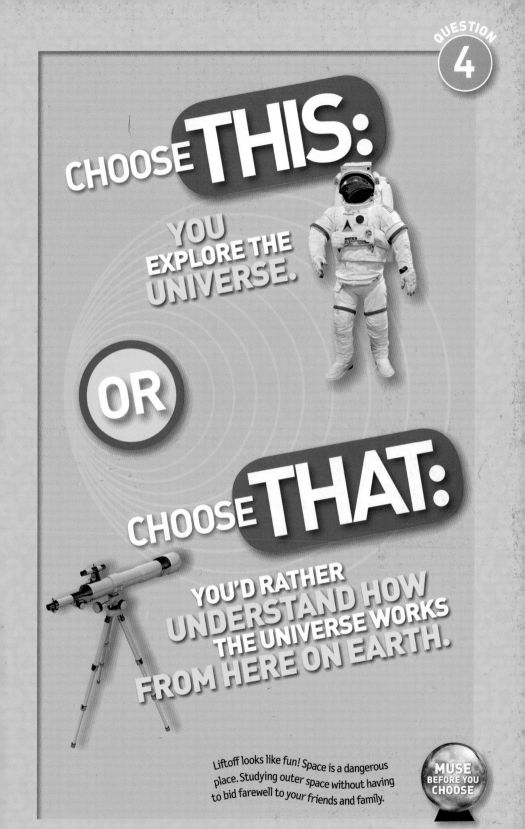

CHOOSE **THIS:**

YOU EXPLORE THE UNIVERSE.

OR

CHOOSE **THAT:**

YOU'D RATHER UNDERSTAND HOW THE UNIVERSE WORKS FROM HERE ON EARTH.

Liftoff looks like fun! Space is a dangerous place. Studying outer space without having to bid farewell to your friends and family.

MUSE BEFORE YOU CHOOSE

53

IF YOU CHOSE THIS:

Prepare for liftoff! The impending popularity of **SPACE TOURISM** means anyone with enough moolah will be able to buy a round-trip ticket to orbit Earth. (Tickets for a flight on Virgin Galactic's SpaceShipTwo start at $200,000 a seat!) If you'd rather take the traditional route to a career in spacefaring (and the Mars One expedition from page 36 is a tad too long-term for your tastes), NASA requires its astronaut candidates to have a bachelor's degree in engineering, biological sciences, physical science, or mathematics. Mission commanders need an additional thousand hours behind the stick of a jet aircraft, so consider joining the Air Force after college to earn your wings. Above all, study hard and never give less than 110 percent—NASA only accepts the best of the best!

IF YOU CHOSE THAT:

Astronauts explore the heavens and astronomers study the objects in them, but **ASTROPHYSICISTS** in particular try to learn how it all fits together. These scientists study the physics of the universe—the visible and invisible forces that rule over space and time. "It's like figuring out a puzzle when you can't actually move or touch the pieces," says Dr. Emily Rice, an astrophysicist at the American Museum of Natural History. "You can only look at them from really far away, and you don't have the box so you don't even know what the puzzle is supposed to look like, or how many pieces there are, or even if you can see all the pieces." If that sounds fun instead of frustrating, then you should start learning everything you can about the universe—its planets, stars, galaxies, and everything in between. Study math, physics, chemistry, and geology in school. Eventually, you'll work with teams of other astrophysicists (it's a group effort) using powerful telescopes and advanced computer simulations to figure out the universe one mystery at a time. "The whole puzzle will probably never be finished," Rice says, "but that means that even small steps are very satisfying."

CHOOSE

THIS:

YOU CAN
**BRING A DOLL
TO LIFE.**

WHERE AM I?

OR

CHOOSE

THAT:

YOU CAN
**CONTROL A ROBOT
WITH YOUR BRAIN.**

**MUSE
BEFORE YOU
CHOOSE**

Making your own friend. What if your
new friend's a jerk? Enhancing your
body with bionics. Dealing with malfunctions.

IF YOU CHOSE **THIS:**

No need to attend any wizardry schools to learn this spell. Instead, study advanced math such as algebra and trigonometry, take programming classes, and get a degree in **COMPUTER SCIENCE.** You'll learn computer languages for writing algorithms—instructions that set the rules in virtual worlds. "Learning an algorithm is just like learning a spell," says Anna Kipnis, senior gameplay programmer with the game company Double Fine. Programmers write these "spells" for everything from handling repetitive tasks (such as programming a robot vacuum to slurp dirt) to breathing artificial intelligence (AI) into video game characters. "Programming an AI character really is like bringing a doll to life," says Kipnis. "You tell it how to think and move and how to react when faced with various situations. If you do it right, it feels like it's alive and actually thinking."

YOU CHOSE **THAT:**

If you're fascinated by the idea of merging humans and machines, consider a career in **BIOMEDICAL ENGINEERING.** By studying how the brain controls the body and can interface with technology, biomedical engineers hope to replace lost limbs and eyes with bionic ones, treat spinal cord injuries, and implant the body with sensors to monitor overall health. "For instance, we're trying to use brain signals recorded from electrodes on someone's head to control an exoskeleton that helps them walk," says Dr. Brian D. Schmit, a professor of biomedical engineering at Marquette University. Like any engineering career, this one requires intensive study of math and science. "To do it right," Dr. Schmit says, "it also requires creativity and a compelling desire to help people."

DIY Developers...

Playing a lot of video games won't get you far if you want to program them. You'll need to practice **MAKING** games, too. "My best advice is to make a game in one of the premade engines like GameMaker, Construct 2, Stencyl, and Unity in your free time," says Kipnis. "You'll learn a lot—and it's really fun."

CHOOSE **THIS:**

RELY ON YOUR SUPERIOR
ATHLETIC ABILITIES
TO CATCH **BIG AIR.**

OR

CHOOSE **THAT:**

RELY ON YOUR SUPERIOR
HAND-EYE COORDINATION
TO CATCH **BIG AIR.**

**MUSE
BEFORE YOU
CHOOSE**

Unlimited adrenaline rushes. Hard landings.
Flight school sounds fun. Airsickness.

IF YOU CHOSE **THIS**:

Skiing, snowboarding, BMX bicycling, surfing, skateboarding, wakeboarding—all the so-called **ACTION SPORTS** feature star athletes who thrill audiences with their high-flying skills and derring-do. Joining their ranks—or "going pro"—is no easy feat. The biggest stars start when they're little. Gold-medalist snowboarder Shaun White was already an expert skier when he switched to snowboarding at age six. Wannabe action-sports pros need to practice, practice, practice and compete in local competitions. Win consistently and you might attract the attention of a sponsor—a company that will give you free gear and (if you're good enough) actually pay you money to have fun at your favorite sport! Just expect to get some bumps and bruises along the way. "Injuries are challenging, but there's always a lesson behind what happened," says champion snowboarder Jamie Anderson. "They help us learn, grow, and tune into our center."

IF YOU CHOSE **THAT**:

Then you should consider a career aboard a real beast of a flying machine: the **HELICOPTER.** Incredibly complex aircraft, whirlybirds require a great deal more instruction to operate than airplanes, and their cockpits demand more multitasking than your video game controller. "Flying a helicopter is like patting your head while rubbing your stomach," says flight instructor and author Helen Krasner, "but it's also like riding a bike—impossible until you can do it, and then you wonder what was so hard." Once you earn your commercial pilot's license, you'll need a different sort of flexibility: the ability to cope with many different jobs, from teaching people to fly to firefighting to taking passengers out for sightseeing. "There are few long-term helicopter jobs," Krasner says, "so you'll need to adapt to a lot of different situations."

CHOOSE

THIS:

YOU WANT TO

EAT ICE CREAM FOR A LIVING.

OR

CHOOSE

THAT:

YOU'D RATHER
PLAY VIDEO GAMES
FOR A LIVING.

MUSE
BEFORE YOU
CHOOSE

Dessert all day. Cavities and
ice-cream headaches. Strained eyes.
Strained thumbs.

IF YOU CHOSE **THIS**:

Good news: **ICE-CREAM TASTER** is a real career! "Yes, it is a dream job," says John Harrison, who tastes about 60 samples a day for Dreyer's Ice Cream. Using a solid-gold spoon to avoid any aftertaste, Harrison scoops a dab from each sample, lets it warm a few degrees to ward off "brain freeze," then swirls it in his mouth to rate the flavor, texture, and even aroma. Harrison recommends that aspiring tasters get a college degree in dairy science or food science. Also, avoid eating onions, peppers, and other spicy foods that will dull your taste buds. But here's the bad news: Tasters spit out their samples instead of swallowing them. Pigging out would only dull their senses, after all.

IF YOU CHOSE **THAT**:

Sorry to poop on your *Mario Party,* but this dream job might turn into a real nightmare! Although **VIDEO GAME TESTERS** do get paid to play games, they're not exactly shooting for high scores or saving any princesses. Testers are typically assigned one specific part of a game—such as opening all the doors, bumping into every wall, or experimenting with inventory items—to look for game-ruining glitches called "bugs," which they must log in reports while writing extensive notes. The one bright side of this gig: Good game testers may get promoted to game designers. In the meantime, the job's long hours hardly allow for any "extra life" in the real world.

DID YOU **KEEP TRACK** OF EACH THIS AND THAT?

TURN THE PAGE TO SEE WHAT YOUR CHOICES **SAY ABOUT YOU!**

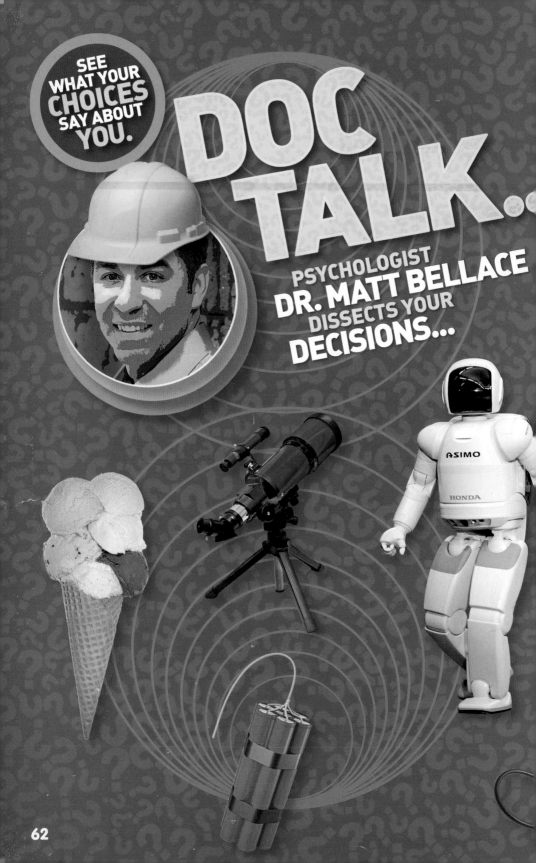

DOC TALK...

PSYCHOLOGIST **DR. MATT BELLACE** DISSECTS YOUR **DECISIONS...**

ASIMO

HONDA

ANALYZE THIS!

CHOOSE THIS, you're what we call a "high-functioning human being." Your personality type likes to be in control, which means you often "run the show." Amazingly, you're a detail-oriented person who is also able to use the creative part of your noodle to solve problems. This is a rare combination! (Many smart people can do one or the other but not both.) You can operate at a genius level while getting some impressive things done. But you're not the complete package—your personal life is probably pretty messy. Hey, you can't have everything!

ANALYZE THAT!

If you mostly picked **CHOOSE THAT,** you're truly an intellectual type who enjoys being a deep thinker. You see the risks involved with being too "hands-on," so you'd prefer to exercise your mind from the sidelines. Just because you avoid the spotlight doesn't mean you can't make an impact on the world. You don't make things—you make things better. You take great enjoyment in studying the world and figuring out how to improve it, but you're not in it for the glory.

CHAPTER 4
GROSS
ANATOMY

Ever wanted to be taller? Shorter? More muscular? You've come to the wrong place! This chapter's choices offer a different sort of makeover. Prepare to ponder the benefits of transparent skin, bonus limbs, extra eyes, and other body oddities that are more practical than pretty. Take one last look in the mirror, because change is afoot from your head to your feet.

CHOOSE **THIS:** YOU HAVE A PREHENSILE TAIL.

OR

CHOOSE **THAT:** YOU HAVE A PREHENSILE TONGUE.

MUSE BEFORE YOU CHOOSE

Getting your tail stepped on in line.
Paying a tailor for tail holes. Public nose-licking.
Never have a milk mustache. So long, silverware!

IF YOU CHOSE THIS:

Give yourself a hand. No, really—give yourself an extra hand! A prehensile tail is like a bonus arm on your backside, able to clutch branches and grab goodies. You've probably seen pictures of howler monkeys using their long, skinny tails to dangle from branches, which frees their arms to grab tasty leaves. But lots of other animals have prehensile tails. **OPOSSUMS,** anteaters, kinkajous, the tree pangolin—they're all in the club. You're in cute company!

IF YOU CHOSE THAT:

A prehensile tongue sure comes in handy. Just ask a **GIRAFFE!** These long-necked lickers wield their 18-inch (46-cm) tongues to strip seriously prickly plants. Africa's acacia trees sprout 3-inch (8-cm) spikes as a defense against grazing animals, but a giraffe's tongue is nimble enough to navigate the thorns and grab the leaves. A giraffe can even jam its tongue deep into its own nostrils to retrieve angry ants that occasionally swarm from tree branches.

Glob and Grab...

If the thought of slurping ants from your nose doesn't turn you off to a prehensile tongue, consider this other nasty giraffe habit: Their mouths generate great gobs of slobber to neutralize toxins in tree leaves.

CHOOSE
THIS:
YOUR HEAD
HAS A BUILT-IN
HELMET.

OR

CHOOSE
THAT:
YOUR BELLY
HAS A BUILT-IN
SUITCASE.

Farewell, hat collection. Mom putting you
in charge of smashing soda cans with your head.
Siblings always asking you to carry their books.

MUSE
BEFORE YOU
CHOOSE

IF YOU CHOSE **THIS**:

Built-in head protection doesn't have to look hideous. Consider the **WOODPECKER.** This handsome headbanger spends the day drumming away on tree trunks hunting for insects. Scientists suspected woodpeckers must have hard heads to put up with all that pecking, and they were right! Scans of woodpecker skulls revealed spongy plate-like bones that absorb impact like a bike helmet. They even have a special bone that wraps around the skull and acts as a sort of seat belt for the brain. Such specialized skulls have inspired the designs of helmets for humans.

Woodpecker head imaged by high-resolution x-ray specimen scanner

IF YOU CHOSE **THAT**:

Now you and a marsupial have matching luggage. A **MARSUPIAL** is a type of mammal that nurtures its vulnerable newborns in a pouch outside its body. Koalas, opossums, and Tasmanian devils all belong to this group of mammals, but none of them display their natural knapsack as prominently as kangaroos and wallabies do. Sometimes, older and younger kangaroo offspring—called joeys—will squeeze into the same pouch. Bet you'll never complain about your room being cramped again.

Talk About an Airhead!

A Swedish duo designed the Hövding, a stylish collar that works like an air bag for your skull. Take a tumble on your bike and—*poof!*—the collar instantly inflates into a head-protecting hood.

CHOOSE **THIS:** YOUR SKIN IS COVERED IN TEETH.

OR

CHOOSE **THAT:** YOUR TEETH ARE COVERED IN HAIR.

MUSE BEFORE YOU CHOOSE

Shredded shirts. Predators fear you. Inventing new hairstyles. *Bleccch*—shampoo!

IF YOU CHOSE THIS:

You'd think that having skin coated in fine fangs would be a real drag, but not if you're a shark. Quite the opposite, in fact! Instead of scales, a shark's skin is armored with itty-bitty teeth called dermal **DENTICLES.** These overlapping, diamond-shaped ridges point toward the shark's tail, reducing drag and boosting swimming speed. They work so well that Olympic swimsuit makers incorporated denticle designs in their fabrics. Now you can slip on your own suit of tiny teeth! Unlike a real shark's denticles, however, the swim fabric won't slice your hand if you rub it the wrong way.

IF YOU CHOSE THAT:

You can't complain if you find a hair in your lunch if you're a **BALEEN WHALE.** These types of whales, which include the humpback, minke, and biggest-of-all blue whale, use their hairy teeth to *catch* lunch. The teeth are actually furry plates that line their massive mouths. Made of keratin—the same substance in human fingernails and hair—these baleen plates act as strainers to filter tiny shrimplike creatures called krill from the ocean into the whales' bellies.

Krill

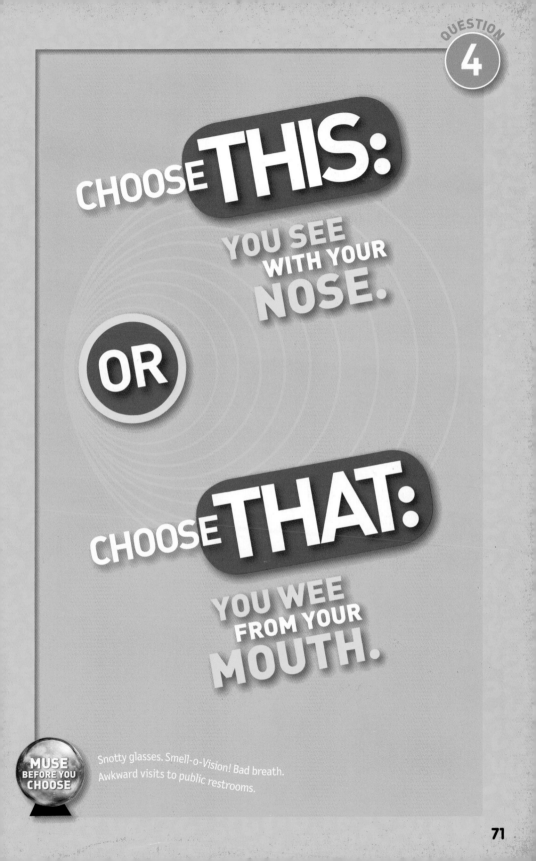

CHOOSE THIS:

YOU SEE WITH YOUR NOSE.

OR

CHOOSE THAT:

YOU WEE FROM YOUR MOUTH.

MUSE BEFORE YOU CHOOSE

Snotty glasses. Smell-o-Vision! Bad breath. Awkward visits to public restrooms.

IF YOU CHOSE THIS:

Then you and a **STAR-NOSE MOLE** would really see eye to eye—or at least nose to nose. This beady-eyed burrower is named for its unusual schnoz, a fleshy bulb bristling with 22 squiggling tentacles. The mole mashes these feelers against tunnel walls to create a three-dimensional mental image of its pitch-black surroundings. The nose knows when it brushes against an earthworm or insect. The feelers grab tight and shove the tasty treat into the mole's mouth.

IF YOU CHOSE THAT:

At least have the decency to hide your head in a puddle when you piddle—just like a **SOFT-SHELLED TURTLE!** Researchers discovered that a species of these turtles in China gets rid of urea (the main waste fluid in pee) from their mouths into puddles rather than from their backsides. This icky habit is actually an adaptation to life in the turtles' brackish—or seawater-tainted—swimming holes, where the water is too salty to flush out waste the old-fashioned way.

CHOOSE

THIS:

YOU HAVE
A SEE-THROUGH
HEAD.

OR

CHOOSE

THAT:

YOU HAVE
A TRANSPARENT
BELLY.

Never hiding what's on your mind.
Sneaking a snack becomes an impossible mission.
Expect screams at the beach.

MUSE
BEFORE YOU
CHOOSE

Heads Up
The barreleye's eyes sit inside its transparent head like twin astronauts in a domed spaceship. The eyelike spots at the front of its head are actually the fish's nostrils.

IF YOU CHOSE THIS:

Psst—your brain is showing! But that freaky head of yours has nothing on the see-through dome of the **BARRELEYE FISH.** This six-inch (15-cm) creature of the deep Pacific not only has a transparent noggin, its orblike eyes are *inside* its head! The barreleye hovers at the inky depths below 2,000 feet (600 m), staring upward through its own skin for the silhouettes of prey. Spooky? Absolutely. Which explains the barreleye's alternate name: the "spookfish."

IF YOU CHOSE THAT:

You better watch what you eat, because everyone else will be watching what you digest. ("Pizza for breakfast again? Lucky!") For a preview of your new see-through anatomy, take a peek inside Costa Rica's **GLASS FROGS.** The bellies of these thumbnail-size frogs are transparent, providing a real-time x-ray of their inner workings. You can see each frog's digestive tract and other organs, blood vessels, green bones—even its tiny beating heart! One thing's for sure if you had similar skin: Everyone would know you have guts!

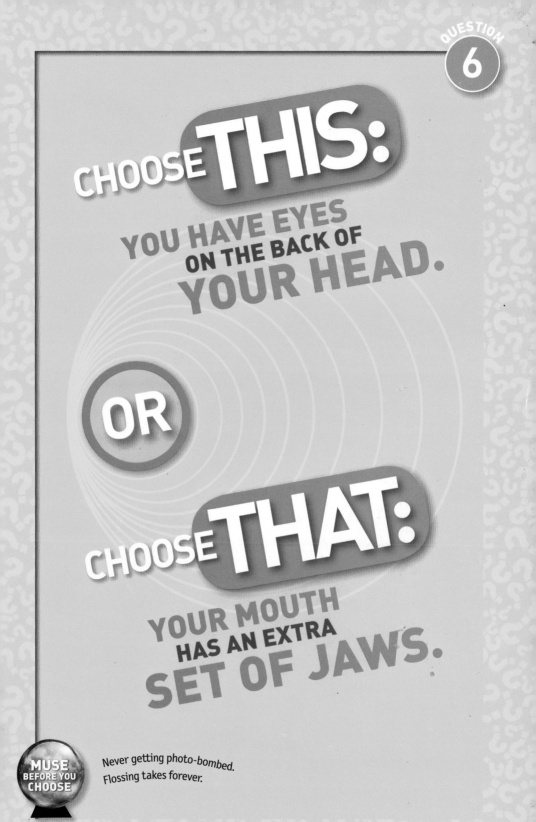

CHOOSE **THIS:**

YOU HAVE EYES ON THE BACK OF YOUR HEAD.

OR

CHOOSE **THAT:**

YOUR MOUTH HAS AN EXTRA SET OF JAWS.

MUSE BEFORE YOU CHOOSE

Never getting photo-bombed.
Flossing takes forever.

IF YOU CHOSE THIS:

Your little brother will never sneak up on you again. But why stop at four eyes when you can have eight? Just look at the **JUMPING SPIDER**—because it's certainly looking at you! These spiders have superperipheral vision: two primary eyes facing front, two pairs on each side of their heads, and a pair facing backward. Fearsome hunters, these spiders lock onto prey with their powerful peepers before pouncing up to 50 times the length of their bodies. They're curious little crawlers, too. Researchers have learned jumping spiders like to watch TV. Their favorite shows: nature programs starring bugs, of course.

IF YOU CHOSE THAT:

Then head to Hollywood. You have a mouth made for sci-fi horror movies! But you don't need to look for space monsters to find a creature with kindred canines. **MORAY EELS** have a second set of jaws—called pharyngeal jaws—deep in their throats. When an eel chomps down on a fish with its main set of choppers, the secondary jaws spring forward and pull the prey deeper into the throat. The two sets of jaws work together to swallow prey faster.

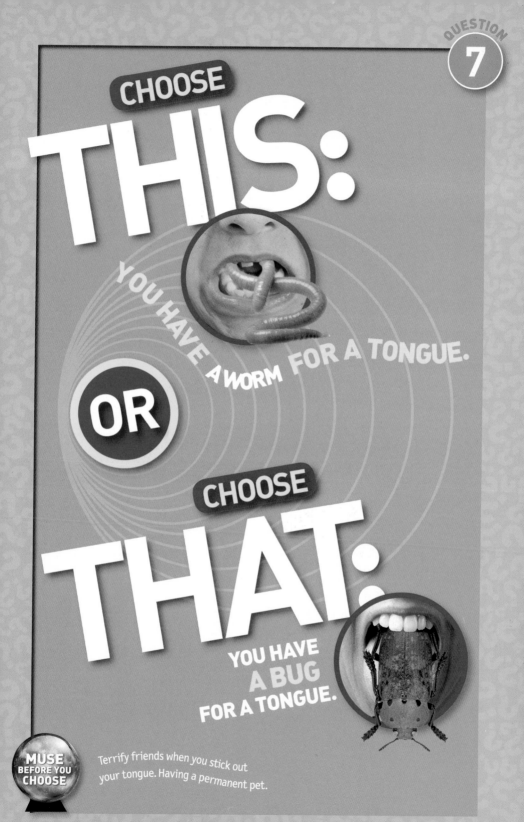

CHOOSE

THIS:

YOU HAVE A WORM FOR A TONGUE.

OR

CHOOSE

THAT:

YOU HAVE A BUG FOR A TONGUE.

MUSE BEFORE YOU CHOOSE

Terrify friends when you stick out your tongue. Having a permanent pet.

IF YOU CHOSE THIS:

Having a worm for a tongue has its benefits. For starters: You can catch all the fish you want without lifting a finger—or a claw, in the case of an **ALLIGATOR SNAPPING TURTLE.** The turtle's tongue isn't actually a worm; it's just shaped like one. While lazing at the bottom of a river or lake, the turtle opens its powerful jaws wide and waggles its skinny red tongue tip. When a hungry fish creeps close to catch the "worm"—snap! The trap is sprung and dinner is served.

IF YOU CHOSE THAT:

Then you must have fallen victim to the **TONGUE-EATING LOUSE!** This creepy crustacean wriggles through the gills of an unsuspecting fish, then slurps all the fluids from the fish's tongue until it withers away. With nothing left to feed on, the louse clutches to the shriveled tongue and actually replaces it, continuing to feed on its host's blood and mucus. Fortunately, the fish doesn't seem to mind that its tongue has been replaced by a monster.

DID YOU **KEEP TRACK** OF EACH **THIS** AND **THAT**?

TURN THE PAGE TO SEE WHAT YOUR CHOICES **SAY ABOUT YOU!**

SEE WHAT YOUR **CHOICES** SAY ABOUT **YOU.**

DOC TALK...

PSYCHOLOGIST
DR. MATT BELLACE
DISSECTS YOUR
DECISIONS...

ANALYZE THIS!

CHOOSE THIS, you've got the right stuff
If you mostly picked for contact sports. You've never shied away from a dodgeball game, and the spike is your favorite volleyball move. When you don't feel like breaking a sweat, you're still watching sports on TV or playing the warrior in your favorite video game. You may be a real peach in person, but choices like armor for your head, spikes in your skin, and eyes protected by your noggin are all signs you're gearing up for action. You've also got a sense of humor. Catching food with your tongue and grabbing things with your tail is hilarious at the school lunch table. Sure, the adults will be horrified, but that makes it even more fun.

ANALYZE THAT!

CHOOSE THAT, then you're fun and
If you mostly picked a little freaky. You see the comedy in hiding creatures in your gut pouch, letting a bug run your tongue, and showing the world how you digest lunch. But you like pushing the limits of comedy—perhaps a little too far sometimes. Some may describe you as impulsive, which explains why you chose a second jaw to chew food you missed the first time, but you prefer the term "unique."

CHAPTER 5
MISADVEN- TURES

"It's a beautiful day," your parents say. "Go play outside." Good idea, but why stop at just stepping outdoors when you can do something outrageous? Swim with a shark the size of a bus! Take a nap strapped to the side of a cliff! Or not. The choices are yours in this chapter that sends you to the limits of your comfort zone—and beyond.

CHOOSE **THIS:**

TAKE A NAP
SUSPENDED
3,000 FEET (915 M)
ABOVE THE
GROUND.

OR

CHOOSE **THAT:**

TAKE A NAP SUSPENDED
230 MILES
(370 KM)
ABOVE THE EARTH.

MUSE
BEFORE YOU
CHOOSE

Forgetting your teddy bear. Do you sleepwalk?
Spectacular views. Fear of falling keeping you up.
Sensation of free fall making you upchuck.

IF YOU CHOSE **THIS**:

Trying to snooze on the sheer side of a cliff might sound like a nightmare, but mountain climbers do it all the time. After an exhausting day spent scrambling up ropes and rock ledges, they crawl into special suspended tents called **PORTALEDGES** and settle in for the night. "They're actually more comfortable than tents on the ground because you don't have any rocks sticking in your back," says adventure photographer Gordon Wiltsie. "You just have to be careful when you cook with the stove. It would be a disaster if the tent burned up around you!" Fortunately, climbers prone to sleepwalking wouldn't fall far if they tumbled out the exit. "You sleep in your harness and never untie it," Wiltsie says. "That's a basic rule of climbing."

IF YOU CHOSE **THAT**:

At least you don't have to worry about falling at this altitude—or even falling asleep on your arm. Here in Earth's orbit, astronauts don't have to worry about gravity at all. But weightlessness presents its own burdens for sleepy spacefarers. If they don't lash their limbs to bulkheads or zip themselves into sleeping bags, snoozing astronauts will drift around the spacecraft's cabin, resulting in painful bumps in the night. Some crew members even use Velcro to strap their pillows to their heads. Try that at your next slumber party!

CHOOSE

THIS:

BEFRIEND AN ALIEN AND SHOW IT AROUND EARTH.

OR

CHOOSE

THAT:

HOP ABOARD A UFO AND NEVER RETURN HOME.

Having to explain reality television. Alien slime everywhere. Always winning the science fair. Exploring the universe. Asteroids!

MUSE BEFORE YOU CHOOSE

IF YOU CHOSE **THIS**:

Let's hope your alien buddy has a better experience with Earthlings than our last alleged interstellar visitors. In July 1947, an unidentified flying object crashed in the desert outside **ROSWELL, NEW MEXICO, U.S.A.** Military officials insisted it was just a weather balloon, but conspiracy theorists later accused the government of hushing up a flying-saucer crash and spiriting away the bodies of the alien pilots for secret experiments. The lesson here: Make sure your otherworldly pal keeps a low profile.

IF YOU CHOSE **THAT**:

Head to State Route 375 near Rachel, Nevada, U.S.A.—perhaps the best spot on Earth to hitch a ride from a flying saucer. Nevada designated this 98-mile (158-km) byway as the **EXTRATERRESTRIAL HIGHWAY** after so many motorists reported UFO sightings. It runs near the supersecret Area 51 airbase, where the military tests experimental aircraft reverse-engineered from crashed flying saucers—or so conspiracy theorists claim.

Close Encounters. . .

How likely is life *out there?* The discovery of hundreds of worlds beyond our solar system—called exoplanets—has left astronomers less skeptical about the possibility of alien life. Even our planetary neighbor Mars had the conditions to support life long ago. Who knows? Perhaps an alien kid elsewhere in the galaxy is wondering if *you* exist.

CHOOSE **THIS:**

GO
BIGFOOT
HUNTING.

OR

CHOOSE **THAT:**

EMBARK ON
A QUEST FOR
A UNICORN.

Tracking 20-inch (51-cm) footprints.
Wait, is Bigfoot friendly? Finding a fairy-tale animal.
Those unicorn horns look pretty sharp.

MUSE
BEFORE YOU
CHOOSE

IF YOU CHOSE **THIS:**

Better begin your search in the Pacific Northwest, supposed stomping grounds of the legendary apelike creature known as **BIGFOOT.** This region includes northern California, Oregon, and Washington, in the United States, as well as the Canadian province of British Columbia. Campers, hikers, and hunters have reported thousands of sightings of Sasquatch—Bigfoot's Native American name—in the region's hilly wilderness. Believers in Bigfoot estimate that as many as 6,000 of the hairy beasts exist in the wild. Keep an eye out for prints left by the creature's size-20 foot, but you'll also need to follow your nose. Bigfoot sightings are often preceded by a big stink (like rotten eggs, but worse).

IF YOU CHOSE **THAT:**

Don't bother searching for the mythical unicorn in some fantasy forest—or even on land. Instead, you'll need to head north to the Arctic Ocean for a guaranteed encounter with an enchanting horned creature. Off the coasts of Russia and Greenland, you'll see a familiar spiraled horn poking above the icy waters. It belongs to the **NARWHAL,** the unicorn of the sea! Male members of this porpoise species grow a swordlike horn—actually a tooth—up to 8.8 feet (2.7 m) long. These tusks were once peddled as magical unicorn horns to gullible Europeans in the Middle Ages.

Seeing Is Believing...
For a surefire sighting of supposed Sasquatch evidence, head to the International Cryptozoology Museum in Portland, Maine, U.S.A. It features photos, eyewitness reports, and even alleged fur samples of Bigfoot, along with exhibits on other "cryptids"—legendary beasts such as the Loch Ness Monster.

CHOOSE **THIS:**

GET LOST.

OR

CHOOSE **THAT:**

HUNT FOR OTHERS.

MUSE BEFORE YOU CHOOSE

Peace and seclusion from nosy siblings.
Hunger pains. Lots of "me" time.
The thrill of the chase. Happy reunions.

IF YOU CHOSE **THIS:**

You'll find no easier place to get lost than in a **HEDGE MAZE.** Popular since the 16th century (and portrayed famously in *Harry Potter and the Chamber of Secrets*), these planted puzzles consist of twisting paths between well-manicured shrubs tall enough to obstruct your view of the exit. But which maze is the most amazing? You could try the oldest, at Hampton Court Palace in Surrey, England, where it has befuddled visitors since 1689. Or wind your way through paths that paint fantastical pictures at Richardson Farm in Spring Grove, Illinois, U.S.A. You'll find the longest maze at the Dole Plantation on Oahu, Hawaii, U.S.A. Built from 14,000 pineapple plants, it sprawls for nearly 2.5 miles (4 km). But the most maddening maze of all is at the Longleat House in Wiltshire, England. Navigate nearly 2 miles (3.2 km) of twisting paths to reach the tower in the maze's center. If you get stuck, head to one of the six bridges within the maze for a bird's-eye view of what lies ahead.

IF YOU CHOSE **THAT:**

The easiest way to engage in hot pursuit is to play **HIDE-AND-SEEK**—the bigger the game, the better! But you could round up everyone in your neighborhood and still not come close to trumping a game held in Doha, Qatar, in 2012. More than 1,200 university students and friends from nearby towns gathered to play what turned out to be the world's largest game of hide-and-seek, a certified Guinness World Record.

Technological Treasure Hunt...

Instead of losing yourself, why not go hunting for treasure? "Geocaching" is a sort of high-tech Easter egg hunt in which people throughout the world search for hidden stashes of coins, books, buttons, toys, and other trinkets. Participants need a global-positioning device or smartphone to track the coordinates of more than 800,000 caches (rhymes with "stashes") hidden by other players. Go online for more information.

CHOOSE

THIS:

"YO-HO, YO-HO, A PIRATE'S LIFE FOR ME."

OR

CHOOSE

THAT:

"OH, GIVE ME A HOME WHERE THE BUFFALO ROAM."

Sailing the high seas. Seasickness.
Sharing a cabin with smelly pirates.
Unlimited sarsaparilla. Saddle sores.

MUSE
BEFORE YOU
CHOOSE

IF YOU CHOSE THIS:

Yo-ho—uh-oh! Those Pirates of the Caribbean movies might make life on the high seas look like one swashbuckling adventure after another, but real **BUCCANEERS** had it rough. Lousy food, cramped quarters, dangerous storms, and frequent sea battles were all part of the job in the golden age of piracy from the late 1600s to the early 1700s. The good news is pirates never walked the plank (that's a Hollywood invention), but real-life punishments were even worse. Bad buccaneers were trussed and dragged beneath the ship, a punishment called keelhauling. Instead of searching for buried treasure (another myth), you'll have more fun arraying your speech with *"arrrrs"* during International Talk Like a Pirate Day every September 19.

IF YOU CHOSE THAT:

Saddle up, buckaroo. The American West might not be as wild as it was during the days of Billy the Kid and other 19th-century gunslingers, but it still needs cowboys and cowgirls! Owning your own horse is a requirement for working on the range, and tending cattle—keeping them safe from sickness and predators—is no easy job. You'd be better off sampling saddle life at a **DUDE RANCH** (don't feel left out, cowgirls—"dude" is slang for city slicker). The Hideout at Flitner Ranch in Shell, Wyoming, U.S.A., offers cowpokes the opportunity to ride and rope cattle, with time off to eat campfire chow and snooze under the stars.

CHOOSE **THIS:**

HITCH A RIDE ON

HALLEY'S COMET.

OR

CHOOSE **THAT:**

HITCH A RIDE ON THE

"VOMIT COMET."

Setting foot on a new world. It's a long trip for a tiny ball of slush. Performing zero-gravity gymnastics. That whole "vomit" thing.

MUSE BEFORE YOU CHOOSE

IF YOU CHOSE **THIS:**

Cool your thrusters—you'll have to wait a while. **HALLEY'S COMET,** the most famous of the comets that wander our solar system, drops by Earth every 75 years or so. It's not due for its next visit until July 2061. While a mission to Halley's comet is certainly possible—a paparazzi of sensor-laden unmanned spacecraft buzzed the comet during its last approach in 1986—the surface of this heavenly body is actually not so pleasant. Like all comets, Halley's peanut-shaped nucleus (or core) is essentially a big dirty snowball, barely nine miles (15 km) long by five miles (8 km) wide. As the comet approaches the sun, ice and dust boil from Halley's surface to form the spectacular tail that astronomers see from Earth—which is really the comfiest seat in the solar system for comet spotting.

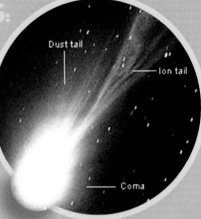

Dust tail

Ion tail

Coma

IF YOU CHOSE **THAT:**

Fasten your seat belts—or, rather, unfasten them—for the world's wildest airplane ride. Daredevil passengers who climb aboard the **G-FORCE ONE** can fly and bounce around the airplane's cabin in zero gravity just like astronauts in space. The modified 727 flies special acrobatic maneuvers that re-create weightlessness for up to 30 seconds at a stretch. Such "reduced-gravity aircraft" aren't new—NASA has been using them for decades to acclimate astronauts to free fall—but a company called the Zero Gravity Corporation is offering civilians a similar experience for $5,000 a ticket. If the price doesn't make your head swim, the ride might. NASA's plane was nicknamed the "Vomit Comet" because two-thirds of the passengers tossed their cookies during flight.

zero G

CHOOSE
THIS:

HOP IN THE OCEAN WITH SHARKS THE SIZE OF WHALES.

OR

CHOOSE
THAT:

DRIFT IN THE SHALLOWS WITH "SEA COWS."

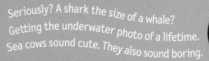

Seriously? A shark the size of a whale?
Getting the underwater photo of a lifetime.
Sea cows sound cute. They also sound boring.

MUSE
BEFORE YOU
CHOOSE

IF YOU CHOSE **THIS**:

Strap on your dive mask and splash around with **WHALE SHARKS,** the world's largest fish. Although they grow to a size rivaling that of a humpback whale, whale sharks are peaceful beasts. They have a mouth that could swallow you whole and thousands of tiny teeth, but they'd rather sift pinhead-size plankton through their gills than gobble up curious swimmers. Their skin—the thickest of any animal—is covered in constellations of yellow spots that are unique to each animal. These elusive sharks roam in tropical seas around the world, but they're easiest to find off Mexico's Holbox Island, where they gather to feed each summer.

IF YOU CHOSE **THAT**:

MANATEES are better known as sea cows for their constant aquatic grazing, but a more suitable nickname might be "sea teddy bear." Lacking natural predators, these half-ton (450-kg) distant relatives of elephants aren't skittish around humans. See for yourself in Crystal River, Florida, U.S.A., the only place in the world where you're guaranteed to see manatees swim by. These docile endangered giants migrate to the river each winter to keep warm in the spring-fed waters. (Despite their blubbery appearance, manatees lack insulating fat.) Unfortunately, their incautious nature puts them in danger from boat impacts and entanglement in fishing nets.

A Whale of a Time...
Landlubbers prone to seasickness can skip the boat trip off Holbox Island and swim with whale sharks in Atlanta at the Georgia Aquarium, one of the world's largest aquariums.

DID YOU **KEEP TRACK** OF EACH THIS AND THAT ?

TURN THE PAGE TO SEE WHAT YOUR CHOICES SAY ABOUT YOU!

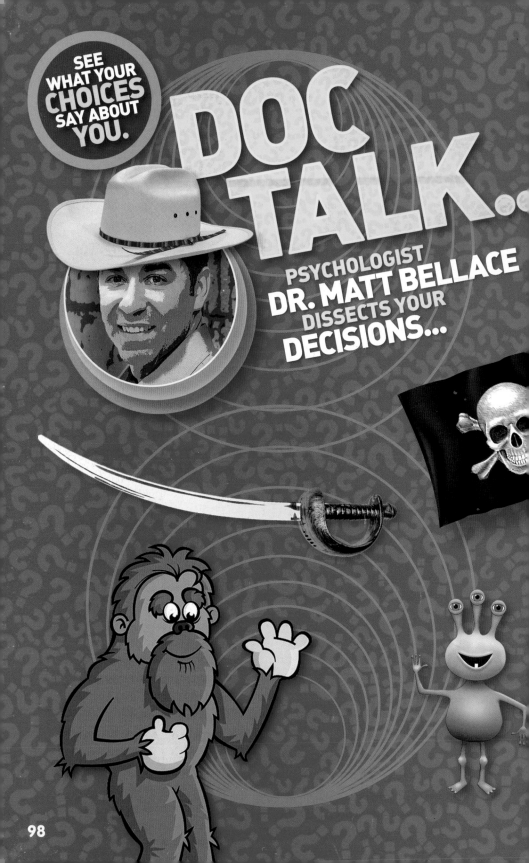

ANALYZE THIS!

CHOOSE THIS, you're a dreamer who finds If you mostly picked books and video games more appealing than real life. This makes you an imaginative and thoughtful person, which are both great qualities. However, you like to be "in your own head," and that can be a problem when you're supposed to be "paying attention." Your favorite games involve taking long journeys or constructing complex cities that you and your "friends" enjoy exploring. Let's hope those friends aren't just virtual, because the downside to your creative mind is a lack of social interaction. Remember, social support is a key to happiness. Real friends need to play a role in your real life!

ANALYZE THAT!

CHOOSE THAT, your personality is geared If you mostly picked toward real-life action and adventure. One of your favorite quotes is "If you're bored, you're boring." Unfortunately, that means you're more likely to need the occasional bandage compared with buddies who spend their time in front of the video game screen. Your choices suggest that you lack the healthy sense of fear that keeps so many of your friends plopped on the couch. This willingness to explore is what makes you interesting and puts you at risk. Play it smart and safe, young daredevil, and you will have a long, exciting existence.

CHAPTER 6
FRIEND ZONE

Beware! You're about to tread into the dreaded territory of classroom cliques, embarrassing secrets, gossip, lies, fitting in, feeling left out, and the dos and don'ts of interpersonal relationships. Don't panic! The social situations you'll ponder here are more fun than serious (well, mostly). And unlike your school quizzes, there's no right or wrong answer to these questions.

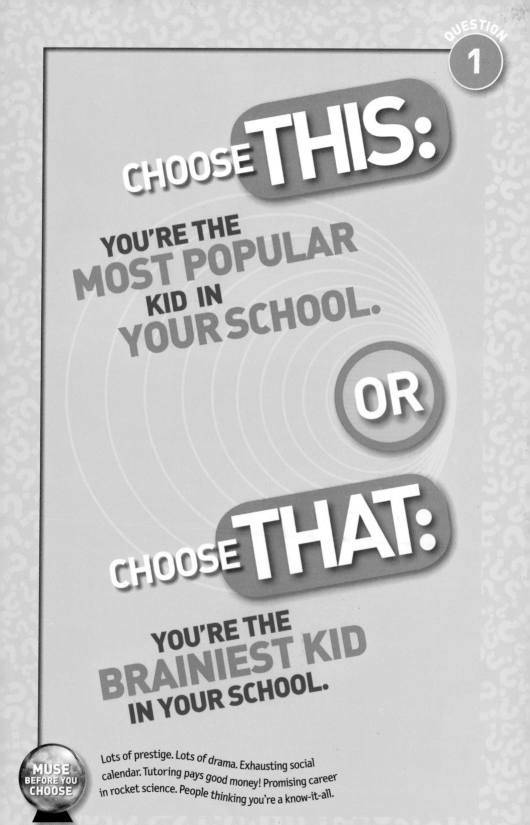

CHOOSE **THIS:**

YOU'RE THE **MOST POPULAR** KID IN YOUR SCHOOL.

OR

CHOOSE **THAT:**

YOU'RE THE **BRAINIEST KID** IN YOUR SCHOOL.

MUSE BEFORE YOU CHOOSE

Lots of prestige. Lots of drama. Exhausting social calendar. Tutoring pays good money! Promising career in rocket science. People thinking you're a know-it-all.

IF YOU CHOSE THIS:

Hey, it just might pay to be **POPULAR**—at least according to a 2012 study by the National Bureau of Economic Research. The study showed that high school students who ranked in the top fifth of their class in terms of having the most friends earned up to 10 percent more than those in the bottom fifth nearly 40 years after graduation. Why? The same qualities that make people well liked tend to take them far in their careers. Of course, the key point here is these students were well liked. Friendliness pays off rather than just popularity, and clawing your way to the top of the social ladder by any means necessary might earn you more foes than friends.

IF YOU CHOSE THAT:

Good for you for being ... well, you! "Being **SMART**—or interesting, talented, artistic, fun, or kind—will continue for you when you're grown up," says Alexandra Robbins, author of the books *The Geeks Shall Inherit the Earth* and *The Overachievers: The Secret Lives of Driven Kids.* "But for the popular kids, being popular ends when they graduate from school." Fill your brain instead of your social calendar and you could grow up to be the next Mark Zuckerberg (founder of Facebook and a smart cookie as a kid) or Stefani Germanotta, aka Lady Gaga (also a gifted pupil in school). "Many of the differences that cause a student to be excluded, or on the fringes, or not popular in school are the same traits or skills that others will admire or respect about that person in adulthood," says Robbins.

CHOOSE

THIS:

JOIN A
MOB.

OR

CHOOSE

THAT:

BECOME A
LONE WOLF.

Never getting lonely, but never having
any alone time. Plenty of peace and quiet.
Maybe too much peace and quiet.

MUSE
BEFORE YOU
CHOOSE

IF YOU CHOSE **THIS**:

Not all mobs are mean—at least if you're a **MEERKAT.** These feisty members of the mongoose family live in social groups called mobs on the dusty plains of southern Africa. It's a dangerous place for a squirrel-size mammal, so members of meerkat mobs take turns standing guard as the rest of the gang hunts and plays together. Sentries scramble to the top of the nearest rock or bush, perch upright on their hind legs, and eye the skies for birds of prey. If a hungry hawk or eagle swoops into view, the lookouts bark an alarm. Mob members know what that means: Take cover in the burrow!

IF YOU CHOSE **THAT**:

The life of a lone wolf isn't as cool as it sounds. **WOLVES** are gregarious animals that thrive in family-based packs, but some wander the wilderness without ever finding a mate, while others lose their pack mates to tragic fates. Unable to use pack teamwork to bring down large animals for dinner, lone wolves must settle for easy pickings: birds, beavers, and rodents—mere morsels compared with typical pack feasts. It's a dangerous life, and a lonely one.

COOL 'KATS
Dark circles around meerkats' eyes act as natural sunglasses as they scan the skies for threats.

CHOOSE **THIS:**

WAKE UP
60 YEARS IN
THE FUTURE.

OR

CHOOSE **THAT:**

WAKE UP
25 YEARS IN
THE PAST.

Maybe you'll get to play *Super Mario 3000*. Feeling
really out of the loop. What if your parents are still
boring as kids? Spoiling the end of the *Diary of a
Wimpy Kid* 20 years before it was written.

MUSE
BEFORE YOU
CHOOSE

IF YOU CHOSE **THIS:**

You might notice something strange when you pay your pals a visit in the year 2074: They look awfully young! In the next 20 to 30 years, doctors could begin injecting patients with microscopic medical robots—called **NANOBOTS**—that will swim through your bloodstream like a swarm of mechanical bees, replacing old cells and curing diseases. Routine nanobot injections could increase your life span by hundreds of years. "Through annual checkups and occasional major repairs by nanorobots, your biological age could be restored once a year to a more or less constant age that you select," says nanobot researcher Robert A. Freitas, Jr. But don't be fooled by your future friends' youthful appearance; they're still nostalgic seniors who'd love to reminisce about the good ol' days of clunky smartphones and Nintendo Wiis.

IF YOU CHOSE **THAT:**

Prepare for a serious case of culture shock. Your parents come from a primitive age when people talked instead of texted, looked up stuff at the library instead of Googled it, and played "totally radical" video games with graphics blockier than Lego sculptures. Yet somehow they got by without the perpetual presence—and constant distractions—of cell phones and the Internet. In fact, if you spend enough time poking around the past, you might realize it's not so bad.

CHOOSE

THIS:

YOU'RE TERRIFIED OF TAKING A TRIP TO **THE LIBRARY.**

OR

CHOOSE

THAT:

YOU'RE TERRIFIED OF TAKING A **BATH OR SHOWER.**

You have a legit excuse for skipping homework. The Harry Potter movies just aren't as good as the books. Saving time getting ready for school. Your body odor could peel paint.

MUSE
BEFORE YOU
CHOOSE

IF YOU CHOSE THIS:

Declaring a war against words? You might suffer from **BIBLIOPHOBIA,** or the fear and hatred of books. A bibliophobe's aversion to the printed page extends to literacy in general. That means schoolwork—particularly English, history, and literature classes—could become pretty tricky. And you'll feel left out when all your friends start raving about the next magical book series (at least there's always audiobooks). We could go on, but why torture you with more icky words?

IF YOU CHOSE THAT:

You've come down with a case of **HYDROPHOBIA** (a fear of water) or—even worse—a medical condition called aquagenic urticaria. Sufferers of this rare allergy break out in itchy lumps when they come into contact with water. Either condition could make your social life stink—literally. After all, even close friends will keep their distance when you start to smell like sweat socks from the bottom of the hamper.

CHOOSE THIS: YOU CAN DETECT WHEN SOMEONE IS LYING TO YOU.

OR

CHOOSE THAT: YOU CAN HEAR EVERY BIT OF GOSSIP SAID ABOUT YOU.

Knowing whom to trust. Never feeling like a sucker. Hearing something you don't like. Discovering what your friends really think about you.

MUSE BEFORE YOU CHOOSE

IF YOU CHOSE THIS:

To be honest, it's not that tough to spot dishonesty. You just need to know what to look and listen for.

Pamela Meyer, a fraud expert and author of the book *Liespotting*, lays out seven tips for deception detection:

CONVINCING WORDS: Liars often begin their fibs with phrases like "To be honest" or "I swear to God."

PROPER TALK: Liars tend to use formal grammar ("I did not steal the Oreos!") instead of contractions ("I didn't steal them!").

BODY ODDITIES: Liars struggle to keep their body language and facial expressions in sync with what they're saying.

DOUBLESPEAK: Liars will often repeat your questions or statements to stall for more time.

OUT OF ORDER: Liars will rehearse their lies in chronological order. Ask them to backtrack and they often get lost.

PRIVATE I'S: Fibbers avoid saying the pronoun "I" and referring to themselves in their lies.

DEEP SIGH: Once done spinning their webs of deception, liars often appear visibly relieved. Watch for a change of posture or a nervous laugh.

IF YOU CHOSE THAT:

Get ready for an earful! Researchers have found that between 65 and 80 percent of all conversations could be considered **GOSSIP**—or idle chatter and rumors about people's private lives. Surprised? Don't pretend you've never dished some dirt yourself! But the good news is gossip isn't all bad. According to one study, only about 5 percent of it is mean-spirited. The rest is considered crucial to making people feel connected and establishing the rules for a functional society. Besides, if you were able to eavesdrop on a story about you that was untrue, you could nip that rumor in the bud!

GOSSIP AHEAD

CHOOSE

THIS:

YOU BECOME FAMOUS, BUT AT THE COST OF LOSING YOUR PRIVACY.

OR

CHOOSE

THAT:

YOU ACCOMPLISH GREAT DEEDS, BUT THEY GO LARGELY UNNOTICED BY THE PUBLIC.

MUSE BEFORE YOU CHOOSE

Signing autographs. Mom and Dad always knowing what you're up to. You'd be like a superhero with a secret identity. A little recognition would be nice.

IF YOU CHOSE **THIS**:

Are you sure you're cut out for the celebrity life? When movie stars, pro athletes, and other famous folks are out and about, crews of camera-wielding **PAPARAZZI** tag along hoping to capture the celebs not looking their best. Did you pick your nose? Forget to zip your fly? Smile with spinach stuck in your teeth? You'll get to relive every embarrassing detail of your day on the gossip shows and in the magazines. It's the price you pay for fame.

IF YOU CHOSE **THAT**:

Ah, so you've chosen the life of the **UNSUNG HERO.** You're in good company! Ever hear of Mary Bowser? Joseph Swan? Helen Sharman? Don't feel bad! Bowser posed as a slave to spy on the Confederate White House during the Civil War, but the details of her heroic deeds were lost to history after the war. Swan invented the lightbulb, although Thomas Edison typically gets the credit. And Sharman became the first British woman in space before soon disappearing from the public eye. The names of these overachievers are hardly household words, but that doesn't detract from their amazing accomplishments.

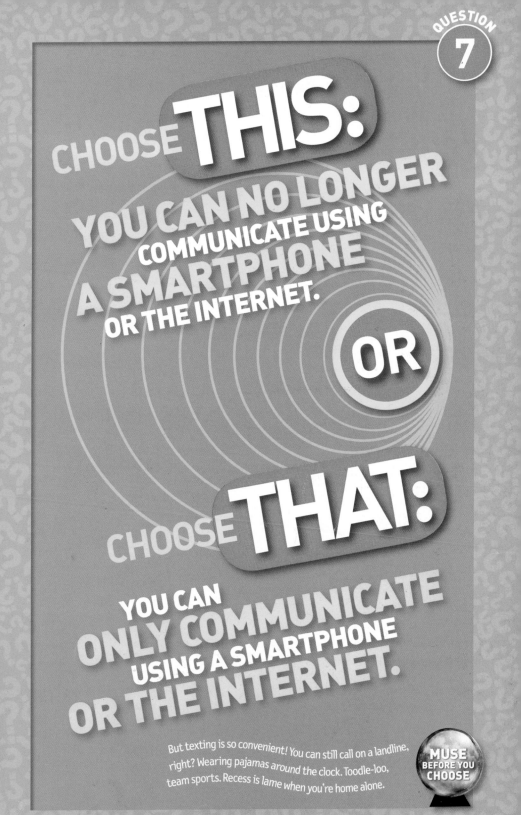

CHOOSE **THIS:**

YOU CAN NO LONGER COMMUNICATE USING A SMARTPHONE OR THE INTERNET.

OR

CHOOSE **THAT:**

YOU CAN ONLY COMMUNICATE USING A SMARTPHONE OR THE INTERNET.

But texting is so convenient! You can still call on a landline, right? Wearing pajamas around the clock. Toodle-loo, team sports. Recess is lame when you're home alone.

MUSE BEFORE YOU CHOOSE

IF YOU CHOSE THIS:

Bid goodbye to texting, Tweeting, instant messaging, social-network updating, and blabbing on your cell phone. Now you're communicating like it's 1985, which means meeting friends face-to-face, corresponding with pen and paper, or calling from a home phone or phone booth. Sounds like a pain, right? But it turns out all these old-fashioned forms of gab might make for a better you. A 2012 study at the University of Winnipeg, in Canada, revealed that frequent texters spend less time reflecting on things and more time obsessing over money and their image. In other words, communicating only in quick digital bursts could make you shallow.

IF YOU CHOSE THAT:

It sounds like what you really need is a robot twin. A company named Double Robotics has developed the **DOUBLE,** a roving robot that serves as your eyes and ears in the outside world when you're stuck in the house. Connect an iPad to the Double's mounting pole, then control your robot stand-in remotely from another iPad or iPhone. The iPad's camera gives you a first-person view while you interact with teachers and friends. It's a poor substitute for face-to-face contact, but at least you can still hang out with your pals!

DID YOU **KEEP TRACK** OF EACH THIS AND THAT?

TURN THE PAGE TO SEE WHAT YOUR CHOICES **SAY ABOUT YOU!**

DOC TALK...

PSYCHOLOGIST DR. MATT BELLACE DISSECTS YOUR DECISIONS...

ANALYZE THIS!

If you mostly picked **CHOOSE THIS,** you're an exceptionally social human being! If Hollywood made a superhero movie in which the hero's power involved social skills, they would be foolish not to cast you. However, like any superhero, you possess vulnerabilities as well as strengths. The upside of being so outgoing is that you find time for a number of social causes. Your ability to do great things for society has no limits. The downside is you can fall victim to a host of social problems, such as getting scammed and blowing off your schoolwork. Use your skills wisely and you could make the world a better place.

ANALYZE THAT!

If you mostly picked **CHOOSE THAT,** you're someone who just might change the world. Your behavior won't always be popular with the masses, but you know that doing your own thing is a key part of being cool. You are comfortable in your own skin, which is why peer pressure has no power over you. Your personality is a bit eccentric, but you enjoy being on your own and "in your own head." Surprisingly, many famous comedians and social-media gurus have a similar style. Like you, they're not overly social beings, but their brilliant ideas have changed how the world interacts.

CHAPTER 7
MAD SCIENCE

Prepare to get a head start in your pursuit of the state of the art. In this chapter you'll choose between scientific breakthroughs that streamline your life or make it more complicated, technologies that exist right now or might very soon, and doodads that save your time or waste it completely. Choose only what you'll use, and remember: New doesn't always mean improved. A few of these technologies might push all your wrong buttons ...

CHOOSE **THIS:**

USE A STAR TREK **TRANSPORTER** TO BEAM ANYWHERE ON THE PLANET.

OR

CHOOSE **THAT:**

USE VIRTUAL REALITY TECHNOLOGY TO EXPLORE FANTASTIC **PHONY WORLDS.**

MUSE BEFORE YOU CHOOSE

You can't blame traffic for being late. Saving a fortune on plane tickets. Power outages leave you sitting in the dark. You'll always need to return to the real world.

IF YOU CHOSE **THIS**:

Imagine zipping to Italy for lunch, zapping to Hawaii for recess, then materializing in math class moments before the bell rings. A **TELEPORTER** would certainly make it easy to get around. Believe it or not, the technology already exists—but it's not quite the crew-beaming transporter from *Star Trek*. Scientists have figured out how to transfer the characteristics of one atom (the basic unit of matter) to a distant atom, a process they call quantum teleportation. It might eventually be used to transmit objects across the solar system. Teleporting people, however, is a trickier matter. The object being teleported is essentially destroyed in one place and duplicated at its destination. Jet lag doesn't sound so bad after all.

Scientists at the U.S. Army Research Laboratory are pioneering data teleportation.

IF YOU CHOSE **THAT**:

VIRTUAL REALITY technology was supposed to offer an escape into lavish computer-generated worlds where anything was possible. Instead, all we got were bulky visors, clunky graphics, and upchuck-inducing motion sickness. A company called Oculus VR might finally deliver on the dream of simulated reality. Its Oculus Rift visor features high-definition displays for each eyeball, creating a three-dimensional wraparound view that shifts with your head movements without any noticeable lag. Game developers have lined up to create virtual worlds for the device.

Oculus Rift visor

CHOOSE

THIS:

DRIVE A
REMOTE-CONTROLLED
ROACH.

OR

CHOOSE

THAT:

DRIVE A
REMOTE-CONTROLLED
SHARK.

Cleaning under the fridge is a breeze. One wrong step and squish! Exploring the deep sea. Goodbye, crowded beaches! What if you lose the remote?

MUSE
BEFORE YOU
CHOOSE

IF YOU CHOSE THIS:

Good news for you (but bad news for any siblings you plan to terrorize with your six-legged minion): Remote-controlled (RC) cockroaches are a reality! By equipping the icky bugs with tiny brain-controlling back-packs, scientists at Tokyo University were able to steer them just like RC cars. Your siblings can rest easy for now, though. The researchers aren't marketing their hot-wired roaches as terrifying toys. Instead, they hope to equip the robo-roaches with cameras and "drive" them into rubble to locate earthquake victims.

IF YOU CHOSE THAT:

It sounds like a triumph of mad science: the ability to control a shark like a toy submarine. A team of marine biologists in Massachusetts, U.S.A., has fig-ured out the trick. They fitted a small shark with electrodes that stimulated the smell cen-ter of its brain. Because sharks always follow their nose, the scientists were able to control their test subject by triggering various odor detectors. Someday, the military might use larger species of remote-controlled sharks as underwater spies.

Shark Sub...
Why drive your shark remotely when you can ride in it instead? A company called Innespace Productions makes the Seabreacher X, a shark-shaped submarine that leaps from the water at 25 miles an hour (40 km/h)!

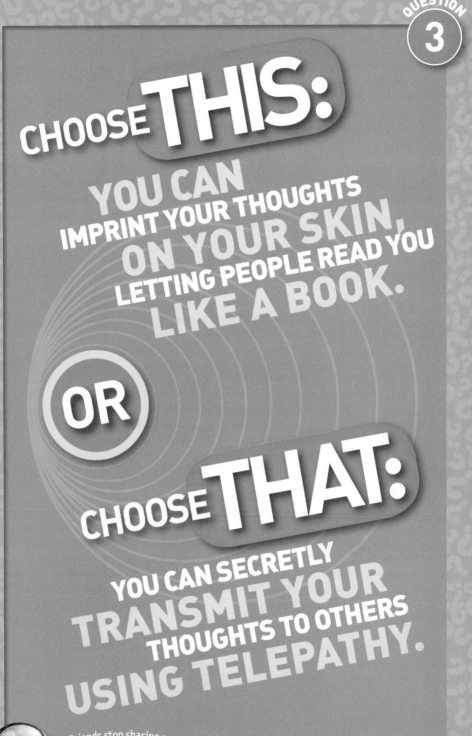

CHOOSE **THIS:**

YOU CAN IMPRINT YOUR THOUGHTS ON YOUR SKIN, LETTING PEOPLE READ YOU LIKE A BOOK.

OR

CHOOSE **THAT:**

YOU CAN SECRETLY TRANSMIT YOUR THOUGHTS TO OTHERS USING TELEPATHY.

MUSE BEFORE YOU CHOOSE

Friends stop sharing secrets. Hiding your crush will be extra hard. Save a fortune on cell phone bills. No more shushing from librarians.

QUESTION 3

IF YOU CHOSE THIS:

Careful what you wish for. If current technology trends continue, skin-mounted **DERMAL DISPLAYS** will turn your forearm into a TV screen in the next few decades. Think of them as animated tattoos. Billions of light-emitting robots implanted under the skin rearrange themselves to display movies, vital health statistics, or whatever's on your mind. Instead of checking e-mail, you'll scan your arm for me-mail!

IF YOU CHOSE THAT:

Thinking out loud will take on a new meaning with the invention of **SYNTHETIC TELEPATHY** devices that transmit thoughts between friends. Sound like science fiction? New York University neuroscientist David Poeppel, as part of his research into thought-reading for the U.S. Army, has created a very simple means of synthetic telepathy using a fridge-size medical scanner that measures brain activity. He says we have a long way to go, but in 50 years we should be able to transmit at least relatively primitive aspects of thinking.

124

CHOOSE

THIS:

RIDE A ROLLER COASTER TO GET AROUND TOWN.

OR

CHOOSE

THAT:

BUILD A ROLLER COASTER IN YOUR OWN BACKYARD.

MUSE BEFORE YOU CHOOSE

Saving gas money. Losing your lunch money—and your lunch—on the way to school. No lines in your backyard. You'll have the most popular house in the neighborhood.

IF YOU CHOSE **THIS:**

Hop aboard the next best thing to a citywide roller coaster. **SHWEEB** is a prototype public-transportation system that suspends riders under a rail in transparent tubes and sends them hurtling along at speeds above 30 miles an hour (50 km/h). If that sounds sluggish for a thrill ride, keep in mind Shweeb is propelled entirely by human power. Riders pedal their pods while clutching handgrips as they bank around turns. The Shweeb system currently exists only in amusement parks, but it may someday supplement buses and trains as an energy-saving way to get around town.

IF YOU CHOSE **THAT:**

For some construction inspiration, take a look at the backyard of Jeremy Reid's parents in Newcastle, Oklahoma, U.S.A. When he was an 18-year-old engineering student—and after asking his dad for permission—Reid began building a **WOODEN ROLLER COASTER** on their ten-acre (4-ha) property. It took him four years to finish his homemade thrill ride, which stretches for 444 feet (135 m) and sends its single-seat car hurtling along at 20 miles an hour (32 km/h). If the ride doesn't make you dizzy, the building costs might. Reid spent $10,000 on his wooden monster.

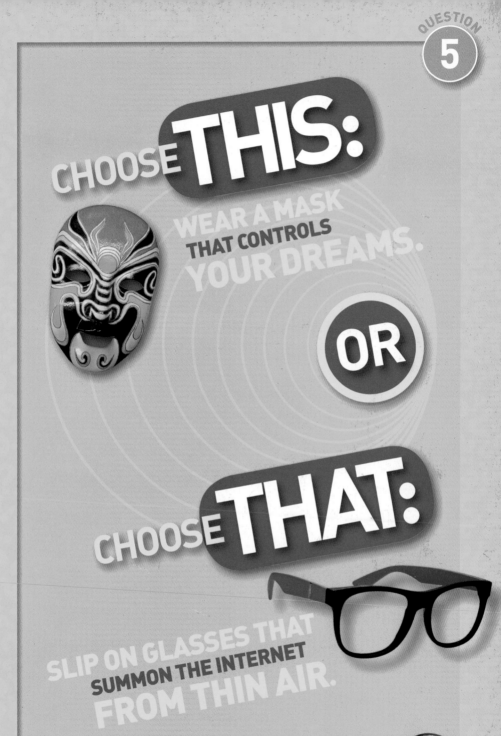

CHOOSE **THIS:**

WEAR A MASK THAT CONTROLS YOUR DREAMS.

OR

CHOOSE **THAT:**

SLIP ON GLASSES THAT SUMMON THE INTERNET FROM THIN AIR.

Soaring like Superman in your sleep. Dreaming right through your alarm. Nerdiest glasses ever. Stumbling over obstacles while watching cat videos online.

MUSE
BEFORE YOU
CHOOSE

IF YOU CHOSE THIS:

Each nap would be an adventure if you could control your dreams. Sleep experts say that the first step to dream mastery is realizing you're actually dreaming. The inventors of the **REMEE SLEEP MASK** claim their product helps you achieve this sort of "lucid dreaming" by flashing lights above your eyelids after you've fallen asleep. The lights appear as unusual patterns in your dreams, telling you that you're dreaming so you can take control of the world around you. What you do next is up to you!

IF YOU CHOSE THAT:

The Internet is everywhere when you slip on **GOOGLE GLASS,** a visor that works like a smartphone for your eyeballs. The visor's eyepiece displays all sorts of handy data—from text messages to Internet search results to your daily schedule. Lost? Just ask the visor for directions and it will project a map to your destination. See something cool? Tell the visor to take a picture—or even a movie—and then share the scene with your friends as you chat with them on the built-in phone. Whatever you see, they see (so be careful to switch off the camera during bathroom breaks).

CHOOSE

THIS:

RAISE YOUR OWN WOOLLY MAMMOTH.

OR

CHOOSE

THAT:

OWN A PET TYRANNOSAURUS REX.

REX

Leash laws. Feeding time. Do they even make a pooper-scooper that big? Potentially disastrous take your pet to school day.

MUSE
BEFORE YOU
CHOOSE

IF YOU CHOSE THIS:

Petting a **WOOLLY MAMMOTH** is a possibility, but you'll need patience. Scientists in South Korea and Siberia (where mammoths once roamed in the thousands) have teamed up to "de-extinct" one of these furry, long-tusked elephant relatives, which have been gone for more than 10,000 years. First, the scientists need to extract cells from frozen mammoth carcasses discovered in the tundra. They'll implant these cells in an elephant, which will act as a surrogate mother for a baby mammoth clone. If all goes well, we could see the return of the woolly mammoth in a matter of years!

IF YOU CHOSE THAT:

Don't believe everything you saw in the movie *Jurassic Park*. Unlike with more recently extinct species such as woolly mammoths, scientists just don't have enough genetic material to resurrect **TYRANNOSAURUS REX.**

But don't give up on your *dino*-mite dreams! A Scottish toy company has created the next best thing—titanic dinosaur toys that come to life. Motors inside each of these "Megasaurs" move its head, wag its tail, and even simulate breathing. Some Megasaurs are life-size, although you better start saving your allowance. The 16-foot (5-m) *T. rex* sells for roughly $10,000.

CHOOSE **THIS:**

CREATE SIMPLE OBJECTS WITH A 3-D PRINTER.

OR

CHOOSE **THAT:**

SPEAK ANY LANGUAGE YOU WANT WITH A UNIVERSAL TRANSLATOR.

Never missing a puzzle piece again. Needing a bigger toy box. Everyone expecting you to order at French restaurants. Becoming the welcoming committee for visiting aliens.

MUSE
BEFORE YOU
CHOOSE

IF YOU CHOSE THIS:

Imagine owning a machine that creates physical objects—from chess pieces to combs to rubber duckies—just like a regular printer duplicates pictures and documents from your computer. A company called MakerBot makes just such a device. Called the **REPLICATOR,** it uses a sort of plastic "ink" to re-create anything from a "Thingiverse" of more than 28,000 simple objects, some as large as a loaf of bread. It's a pioneering piece of technology in a product line that will evolve to create more complex goodies, including other 3-D printers!

IF YOU CHOSE THAT:

World travel is tricky if you can't even ask for directions to the bathroom. Foreign relations will get a lot easier once software company Microsoft perfects its **UNIVERSAL TRANSLATOR.** This high-tech program not only translates your speech into the language of your choice, it also plays your message aloud in your own voice.

> Muy bueno, ¿no? Ahora, ¿dónde está el baño, por favor?*

*Translation: "Very good, no? Now, where is the bathroom, please?"

DID YOU **KEEP TRACK** OF EACH THIS AND THAT?

TURN THE PAGE TO SEE WHAT YOUR CHOICES **SAY ABOUT YOU!**

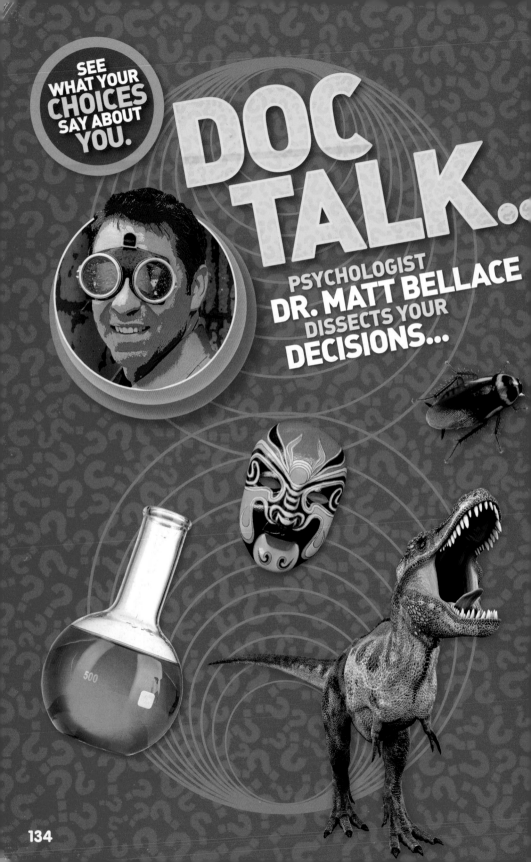

SEE WHAT YOUR CHOICES SAY ABOUT YOU.

DOC TALK...

PSYCHOLOGIST
DR. MATT BELLACE
DISSECTS YOUR
DECISIONS...

ANALYZE THIS!

If you mostly picked **CHOOSE THIS,** you're the type of person who thinks big but is often underwhelmed by reality. What sounds to you like a great idea (e.g., taking a roller coaster to school) turns out be a lot of work (e.g., pedaling in a tube to school). The good news is that your personality style forces you to be a realist. This helps you manage your expectations, so you're happier than the average woolly mammoth.

ANALYZE THAT!

If you mostly picked **CHOOSE THAT,** congratulations are in order. You've got an eye for cutting-edge technology that is not only exciting but totally cool. You're a visionary who also appreciates the power of gadgets that make life easier. The only downside is you tend to look for the easy way out in life. You say things like "Why study for Spanish? I'll just use my universal translator." If you aim for a combination of brilliant ideas and hard work, you could be the next Steve Jobs.

135

CHAPTER 8

OFFBEAT FEATS

Everybody's good at something. Maybe you're a stellar swimmer? A super sprinter? An extreme eater? Whatever your area of expertise, it probably won't get you far with this chapter's challenges. After all, could you outswim a crocodile or sprint across red-hot embers? Prepare to ponder off-putting accomplishments and sickening stunts that just might land you in the record books.

CHOOSE **THIS:**

BECOME
THE BEST
IN THE WORLD
AT SOMETHING.

OR

CHOOSE **THAT:**

BECOME
THE FIRST
IN THE WORLD
AT SOMETHING.

Celebrity status and bragging rights.
Having to practice for thousands of hours. All the best
records are tough to beat—good luck drowning out the
loudest belch!

MUSE
BEFORE YOU
CHOOSE

IF YOU CHOSE **THIS**:

In his famous book *Outliers: The Story of Success,* author Malcolm Gladwell explains that to achieve greatness in any sport, career, or other endeavor, a person needs to put in 10,000 hours of practice. That's more than a year's worth of round-the-clock work! You can give yourself a head start by polishing a particular skill you already excel at or enjoy. Or you can take a shortcut and attempt to topple an easy-to-beat record. Skim the Guinness World Records and you'll find all sorts of funky feats that few have attempted. Think you can break the record for the quickest **100-METER HURDLE** while wearing **SWIM FLIPPERS?** Or run the fastest 10-kilometer race while hula-hooping? Only one way to find out!

IF YOU CHOSE **THAT**:

If you can't break a world record, why not invent your own? The Guinness World Records organization receives more than **50,000 SUBMISSIONS** a year from people eager to break records or create new ones. Register your novel feat at *www.guinnessworld records.com* and then become the first in the world to set a record. Just make sure to read all of Guinness's guidelines before getting too far in the process. It would be a shame to spend an hour eating ice cream in a coffin full of earthworms only to realize that Guinness no longer cares about endurance challenges!

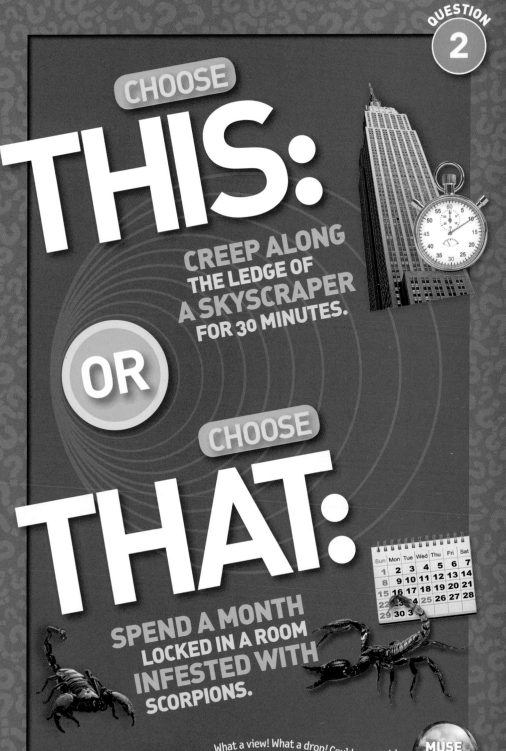

CHOOSE
THIS:

CREEP ALONG THE LEDGE OF A SKYSCRAPER FOR 30 MINUTES.

OR

CHOOSE
THAT:

SPEND A MONTH LOCKED IN A ROOM INFESTED WITH SCORPIONS.

What a view! What a drop! Could you squish all the scorpions? Good luck falling asleep!

MUSE BEFORE YOU CHOOSE

IF YOU CHOSE THIS:

LEDGE LURKING might look electrifying, but it doesn't have to be death defying—at least if you trek to the top of Toronto's CN Tower. Visitors who sign up for an EdgeWalk can stroll along a ledge 1,168 feet (356 m) above the city streets. The walkway is about as wide as a sidewalk and lacks hand-rails. Scary, right? But safety harnesses tethered to the tower keep ledge walkers from toppling off. So unless you're seriously acrophobic (afraid of heights), feel free to lean out and enjoy the view.

IF YOU CHOSE THAT:

Then you clearly don't suffer from arachnophobia—the fear of arachnids such as spiders and scorpions. But even if you tough out a month in a cramped chamber crammed with creepy crawlies, you still wouldn't break the Guinness World Record set by Kanchana Ketkaew, Thailand's "Scorpion Queen." She spent 33 days in an itty-bitty room with more than **5,000 SCORPIONS.** Her arachnid roomies scurried across Ketkaew as she watched TV, read books, ate, and even slept. By the time she emerged, Ketkaew had been stung 13 times!

Walking on Air...
If the thought of going on an EdgeWalk puts a lump in your throat, the Grand Canyon Skywalk offers a more down-to-earth opportunity to stroll where eagles soar. This U-shaped sidewalk extends from the Grand Canyon's rim and offers stunning views in every direction—even straight down. The Skywalk's floor is transparent!

CHOOSE **THIS:**

SPEND 15 MINUTES IN **THIS TANK.**

OR

CHOOSE **THAT:**

SPEND AN ENTIRE NIGHT IN **THIS HAUNTED HOTEL.**

What a croc! Just how thick is plexiglass, anyway? Anything's better than sleeping in that scorpion room on the opposite page.

MUSE
BEFORE YOU
CHOOSE

IF YOU CHOSE THIS:

You think swimming in a cage surrounded by great white sharks is scary? Try going nose to scaly nose with an 18-foot (5.5-m) saltwater crocodile in the **CAGE OF DEATH!** This attraction at the Crocosaurus Cove reptile park in Darwin City, Australia, lets two people tread water for 15 minutes in a giant see-through cylinder that's lowered into the crocodile exhibit. (For maximum terror, dive in during feeding time.) Daredevil swimmers get an up-close look at one of nature's deadliest predators, while the crocodile gets an up-close look at the tasty swimmers. Despite its scary name, the Cage of Death has never hosted an unhappy ending.

IF YOU CHOSE THAT:

Things do more than go bump in the night at the **CRESCENT HOTEL & SPA** in Eureka Springs, Arkansas, U.S.A. Sometimes they send a chill up your spine—or even reach out and grab you! Known as one of America's most haunted hotels, this resort and former hospital is supposedly home to no fewer than eight restless ghosts, including a former patient fond of materializing at the foot of your bed. Guests have reported chilly sensations in their limbs and being tugged by unseen hands. Nightly ghost tours introduce visitors to all of the hotel's spooky spirits, but nothing's stopping you from checking into a room and spending the night. Sweet dreams!

CHOOSE

THIS:

EAT A **SANDWICH** OF **STUPENDOUS SIZE.**

OR

CHOOSE

THAT:

CHUCK CHOW AT THE WORLD'S **LARGEST FOOD FIGHT.**

MUSE BEFORE YOU CHOOSE

Leftovers for life. You'll need a moving van for a lunch box. Stained everything! Exercising as you eat.

IF YOU CHOSE **THIS**:

You'll find no shortage of supersize sandwiches in the record books. Three snack-construction crews in Beirut, Lebanon, once built a submarine sandwich more than four times the size of an actual submarine! But while that hoagie was humongous, it didn't look quite as appetizing as the **3.5-TON** (3,178-kg) ham-and-cheese beast built in Mexico City in 2004. More than 20 sandwich makers crafted a custom oven just to bake the bread, which measured 11.5 feet (3.5 m) on each side. Good luck taking a bite out of that!

IF YOU CHOSE **THAT**:

Put on your nastiest clothes and fly to the Spanish town of Buñol. Here, every August, about 40,000 people gather in the town square for the food-flinging festival of **LA TOMATINA.** Participants spend an entire hour tossing over-ripe tomatoes—an estimated 150,000 of them—at each other until everyone and everything is dripping with sticky juice. Just be glad you don't have to clean *that* up.

Dino-Size Dessert...
If you have a healthy appetite *and* an unstoppable sweet tooth, why not gnaw the walls of a life-size gingerbread house. The world's largest was built in 2006, in the Mall of America in Bloomington, Minnesota, U.S.A. It stood nearly 70 feet (21 m) tall and was assembled from 14,250 pounds (6,464 kg) of gingerbread held together with 4,750 pounds (2,155 kg) of icing, garnished with more than a ton of Tootsie Rolls, Hershey's bars, Twizzlers, and other candies. Talk about a home sweet home!

CHOOSE **THIS:** GO FOR A BAREFOOT STROLL ON HOT COALS.

OR CHOOSE **THAT:** TAKE A DIP IN THE ICY ARCTIC OCEAN.

Blistered toes. Fastest ten-meter (33-ft) dash ever!
B-B-Blue lips. Hot chocolate will never taste better.

MUSE
BEFORE YOU
CHOOSE

IF YOU CHOSE THIS:

Better watch your step! Although fleet-footed dare-devils have been traipsing down paths of glowing embers since at least 1200 B.C. for all sorts of reasons—from rites of passage to corporate team building—**FIREWALKING** is still a risky feat for your feet. Nearly two dozen people blistered their soles at a fire-walking event in 2012. But why doesn't everyone who strolls across coals toast their tootsies? Scientists say that smoldering embers don't transmit heat effectively to the bottoms of fast-moving feet. Firewalking enthusiasts, on the other hand, believe their own self-confidence protects them—a triumph of cool minds over red-hot matter. Regardless, the only sure-fire way to save your soles is to stay off the coals!

IF YOU CHOSE THAT:

No need to charter a ship to the top of the world for a freezing dip. Just watch for a local **POLAR BEAR PLUNGE** to experience some cold-water camaraderie. At these wet-and-wild winter gatherings, like-minded bathers frolic by the hundreds in bone-chilling waters wearing nothing but swim trunks or bikinis. They take the plunge to raise money for charity or just for fun. (Really!) Thousands of people celebrate New Year's Day with a bracing swim at the annual Nieuwjaarsduik, or New Year's Dive, in the Netherlands. Whether you decide to make a big splash or just dip in a toe, always stick with the group for safety.

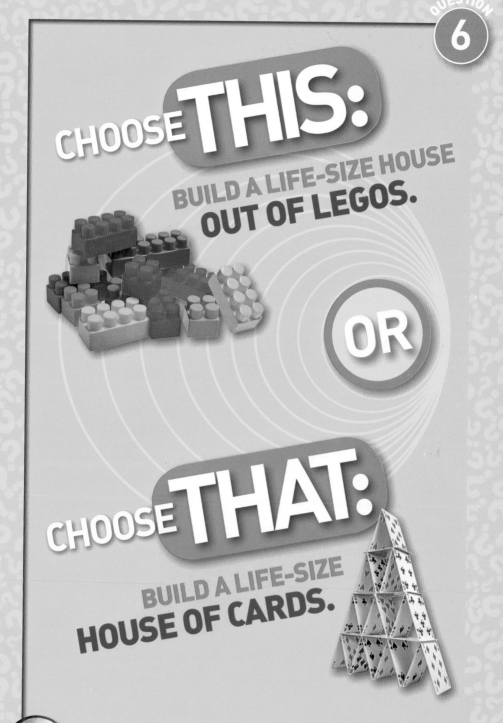

CHOOSE THIS:

BUILD A LIFE-SIZE HOUSE OUT OF LEGOS.

OR

CHOOSE THAT:

BUILD A LIFE-SIZE HOUSE OF CARDS.

MUSE BEFORE YOU CHOOSE

Building is a snap. Legos aren't cheap.
One sneeze would bring down the house.
Demolishing your creation is half the fun.

IF YOU CHOSE **THIS**:

You better have a lot of Legos—at least 3.2 million of them. That's how many bricks British television star James May needed to build a two-story **LEGO HOUSE** in a Surrey vineyard. His snap-together casa had all the comforts of home: windows and skylights, a kitchen complete with dishes and snacks, a king-size bed topped with pillows and sheets, and even a bathroom with a working shower and toilet—all assembled from Lego pieces (yep, even the toilet paper). Whether you'd want to live in a Lego house is another matter. May learned after a sleepless night that his bed wasn't comfy and the ceiling leaked when it rained.

IF YOU CHOSE **THAT**:

Seek construction advice from Bryan Berg, an American architect who holds the Guinness World Record for erecting the tallest **HOUSE OF CARDS,** at 25 feet 9 7/16 inches (7.86 m). Berg advises that card-construction workers use cheap decks that are less glossy—and therefore less slippery. Lay your foundation by holding the first card in your left hand and leaning the second card against it with your right, creating a T shape. Repeat on the opposite side to turn the T into a square, the basic four-sided cell you'll repeat in rows and stacks throughout your entire house.

Living in Legos...

If you lack the patience and pieces to build your own Lego living room, why not check in to a premade pad? The Legoland Hotel in Carlsbad, California, U.S.A., looks like a three-story Lego fortress complete with a dragon and brick-filled moat. Each room is loaded with unique Lego sculptures. Bring your own bricks to add personal touches, and complete your room's treasure hunt to unlock a chest full of surprises.

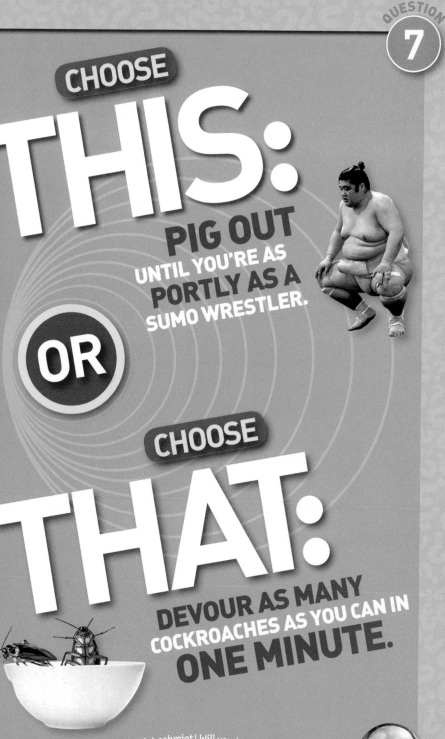

CHOOSE

THIS:

PIG OUT UNTIL YOU'RE AS PORTLY AS A SUMO WRESTLER.

OR

CHOOSE

THAT:

DEVOUR AS MANY COCKROACHES AS YOU CAN IN ONE MINUTE.

Diet schmiet! Will you have to dress like a sumo wrestler, too? It'll all be over in a minute. Icky tickles in your throat.

MUSE BEFORE YOU CHOOSE

IF YOU CHOSE **THIS**:

Don't order that fourth dessert just yet. Despite their blubbery bodies and ground-shaking weight—some weigh in at more than 400 pounds (181 kg)—sumo wrestlers don't spend the day scarfing down junk food. They're athletes, and like any athlete they need to eat right to stay in shape. The breakfast, lunch, and dinner of sumo champions is ***CHANKONABE,*** a protein-rich stew overflowing with beef, vegetables, and fish. Sumos in training consume chankonabe in great quantities to build muscle. They eat heaping side dishes of white rice, then follow each meal with a nap. Snoozing so soon after eating lowers the body's metabolism. All that rice is stored as fat, turning each sumo wrestler into a mountain of a man!

IF YOU CHOSE **THAT**:

There's no shame in ingesting insects. **EIGHTY PERCENT** of the world's population include bugs in their diet! No need to eat the little buggers while they're still squirming, either. Ask an insect chef to sauté them with light seasonings. The flavor of cooked cockroach has been likened to "greasy chicken." Manage to munch more than two dozen roaches in a minute and you'll beat the world record. Bug appétit!

Buggy Beware!
When dabbling in entomophagy (the eating of insects), take care not to bite off more than you can chew. A Florida man died of choking in 2012 after winning a cockroach-eating contest. Oh, and never munch on any insect if you're allergic to shellfish (the bugs of the sea).

DID YOU **KEEP TRACK** OF EACH **THIS** AND **THAT**?

TURN THE PAGE TO SEE WHAT YOUR CHOICES **SAY ABOUT YOU!**

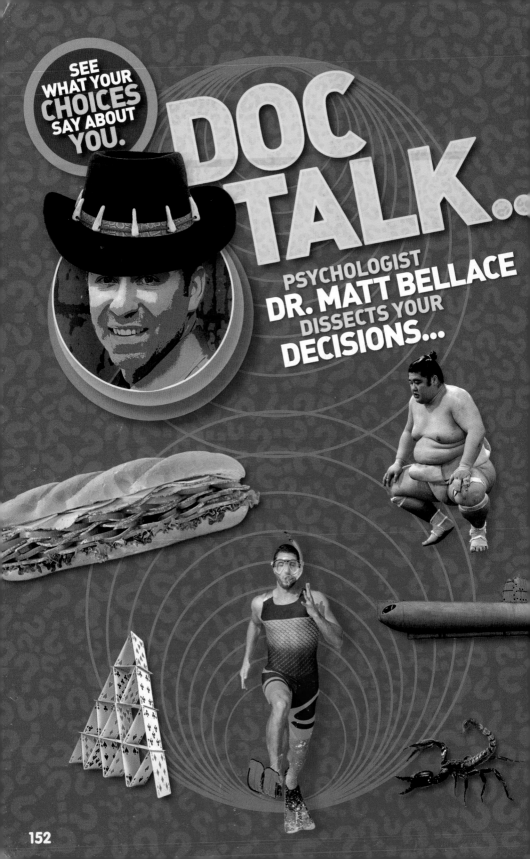

SEE WHAT YOUR CHOICES SAY ABOUT YOU.

DOC TALK...

PSYCHOLOGIST DR. MATT BELLACE DISSECTS YOUR DECISIONS...

ANALYZE THIS!

CHOOSE THIS, you enjoy being different and standing out from the crowd. You live life on the edge (literally, sometimes), but your personality favors calculated risk taking over the more dangerous stuff. For example, you probably love eating hot sauce to impress your friends, but eating a live bug in front of them? Not so much. Scientists say that people with your personality use both sides of their brain equally well, employing logic and emotion as they accomplish amazing feats.

ANALYZE THAT!

CHOOSE THAT, If you mostly picked you're one of those rare people who enjoys getting a few bumps and bruises. It sounds odd, but you get a kick out of pushing your physical and emotional limits. The good news is you are likely to achieve success in life. Research shows that young people who show patience in pursuing their goals and are willing to face challenges head-on will end up more accomplished later in life. Of course, this assumes that you survive your painful pursuits to enjoy the good times!

CHAPTER 9
ABSURD SITUATIONS

You think the previous eight chapters posed some crazy choices? You haven't seen anything yet! Awful afflictions, lose-lose scenarios, sur-real situations—we've saved the silliest for last in this final chapter, the bitter end of *This or That?* Oh, and remember way back in the introduction when we said there were no wrong answers? We were wrong. Beware of trick questions ahead!

CHOOSE **THIS:**

SUFFER FROM A SNEEZING SPREE THAT NEVER CEASES.

OR

CHOOSE **THAT:**

GET A CASE OF THE HICCUPS THAT LASTS FOREVER.

Dirty looks at the salad bar. Getting sick of hearing "gesundheit." Constant shushing at movie theaters.

MUSE BEFORE YOU CHOOSE

IF YOU CHOSE **THIS**:

You're wise not to stifle a sneeze. It's an important bodily function for blasting boogers and other debris from your air passages. But while a lone sneeze is essential, a long fit can be exhausting. Each **AHH-CHOO** involves a mini-workout of the muscles in your face, throat, chest, and abdomen, all working together to expel foreign particles from your nose and mouth at nearly 100 miles an hour (161 km/h). Now imagine the ordeal of Donna Griffiths, a 12-year-old English girl who suffered from a sneezing spree that lasted for 978 days!

IF YOU CHOSE **THAT**:

Never-ending hiccups might seem less annoying than ceaseless sneezing, but consider the life-disrupting consequences of well-meaning friends offering a "cure." Farmer Charles Osborne of Iowa, U.S.A., hiccuped every day for nearly **70 YEARS** (doctors think he damaged the hiccup-controlling part of his brain after straining to lift a heavyweight hog). Before he passed away in 1991, at age 98, Osborne received thousands of letters with homemade remedies. One buddy even fired a double-barreled shotgun just out of sight, hoping to scare away the hiccups.

CHOOSE **THIS:**

LIVE YOUR LIFE AS
HARRY
POTTER.

OR

CHOOSE **THAT:**

SUFFER FROM A
DIFFERENT OBSCURE
PHOBIA EVERY DAY.

PLATFORM 9¾

**MUSE
BEFORE YOU
CHOOSE**

Everybody knows your name. Everybody
wants to see a magic trick, your wand, the
Golden Snitch, your Nimbus 2000, etc. Being
afraid of being afraid.

IF YOU CHOSE **THIS:**

We hate to break your spell, but life as Harry Potter isn't as magical as you might think. Just ask a **REAL-LIFE HARRY.** Born in 1989 in Hampshire, England, Harry Potter lived his early years with an unremarkable name until author J. K. Rowling introduced her Boy Who Lived to the world in 1997. At first, the real Potter thought it might be fun to share a name with the famous fictional wizard. Then came the endless wizarding jokes from classmates, friends, and even teachers. He's had to show his identification to buy bus passes and soccer tickets from clerks who think he's playing a joke. It doesn't help that he looks like Harry Potter—right down to a scar on his forehead (received when he ran into a lamppost at age 15). Now in his 20s, the real Mr. Potter works at a bank. He rarely tells clients his full name.

IF YOU CHOSE **THAT:**

It's no fun living with a phobia, a fear triggered by specific objects, animals, or situations. But suffering from the more obscure scares might not be so terrible. After all, you would never know you woke up with **COULROPHOBIA** (call-ro-foe-be-ah) unless the circus came to town (it's the fear of clowns). **CHIONOPHOBIA** (key-on-oh-foe-be-ah)—the fear of snow—wouldn't affect you if you lived in Hawaii, but then nothing ruins a day at the beach like a bad case of **CYMOPHOBIA** (sime-oh-foe-be-ah), the fear of waves, or **OMPHALOPHOBIA** (omm-fal-oh-foe-be-ah), the fear of belly buttons. The truth is, you're in for some long days with these freaky phobias—especially if you wake up with **HELIOPHOBIA** (heel-ee-oh-foe-be-ah), the fear of sunshine.

CHOOSE

THIS:

MAKE A SANDWICH ON YOUR KITCHEN COUNTER.

OR

CHOOSE

THAT:

MAKE A SANDWICH ON A TOILET SEAT.

Wait, is this a trick question? Bologna on the toilet seat? Seriously, this has to be a trick question.

MUSE BEFORE YOU CHOOSE

IF YOU CHOSE THIS:

Better be wary of where you assemble that sandwich. Studies show that the room in your house devoted to food prep is nastier than the place where you poo! Billions of **BACTERIA** crawl across your kitchen countertops and hide in the knife nicks of your cutting board—typically home to 200 times more doo-doo-related germs than a toilet seat. Cleaning the counters with the dish sponge only spreads the nastiness (salmonella, E. coli, and other germs live in the damp nooks of your sponge, making it the most awful object in your house). So ask your parents for help sanitizing the kitchen once in a while. Vinegar works wonders! In the meantime, make your sandwich on a plate.

IF YOU CHOSE THAT:

Here's a fact that's hard to swallow: Your toilet seat is actually **LESS GERMY** than your kitchen counter. How's that possible? Home dwellers tend to scrub toilets and bathroom floors with bacteria-killing disinfectants, while kitchen countertops just get a quick wipe from the icky dishrag. Bacteria doesn't survive for long on the dry surface of a toilet seat, either. Still, anyone with a healthy immune system has little to fear from household germs, so by all means stick with the kitchen for stacking your bologna. At least now you won't feel so funky when you spot Spot sipping from the toilet.

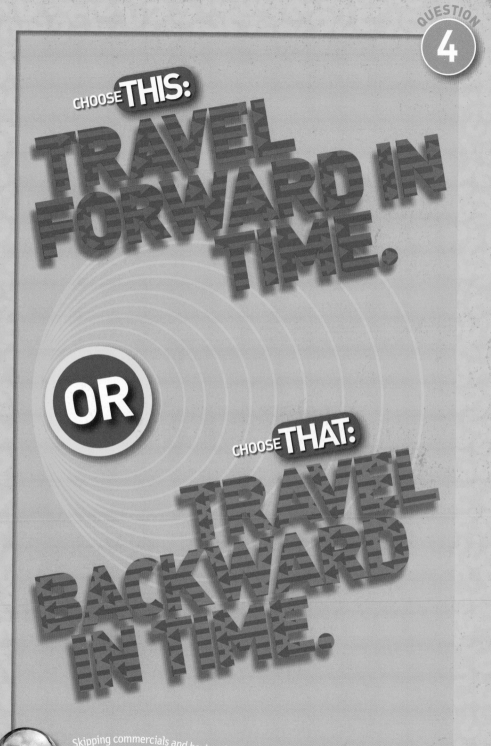

CHOOSE **THIS:**

TRAVEL FORWARD IN TIME.

OR

CHOOSE **THAT:**

TRAVEL BACKWARD IN TIME.

**MUSE
BEFORE YOU
CHOOSE**

Skipping commercials and boring classes.
Extreme culture shock. Meeting your ancestors.
Meeting your younger self.

IF YOU CHOSE **THIS:**

Not only is journeying forward in time possible, humans do it all the time! According to laws of physics that are far too complicated

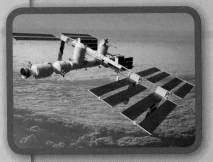

to explain here, time slows down for a person as he or she speeds up. This effect—known as time dilation—is only really perceptible as you approach the speed of light (which is really, really, *really* fast). Astronauts aboard the **INTERNATIONAL SPACE STATION** orbit Earth at 18,000 miles an hour (29,000 km/h), which is just a tiny fraction of light speed, but they're still moving fast enough to experience time dilation on a measurable scale. When they return home from a six-month assignment, astronauts are actually .007 seconds younger than their friends and family on Earth. In other words, they've traveled a fraction of a second into the future!

IF YOU CHOSE **THAT:**

Ah, you've chosen the trickier type of time tripping. Physicists fear that traversing the time line in reverse would lead to paradoxes: Situations that would prevent you from making the journey in the first place. Imagine if you accidentally hit your grandpa with your time machine or prevented your mom and dad from going on their first date? If you had never been born, you wouldn't have traveled back in time to begin with, right? Some astrophysicists believe the universe protects itself from such paradoxes by making backward time travel impossible. Others believe that trips to the past are theoretically possible via **WORMHOLES**—

galaxy-spanning shortcuts that exist only in scientific papers (for now). Even if you could harness the vast energies needed to safely enter a wormhole, you might end up in a parallel universe identical to our own but with its own separate time line. Maybe it's best to just stick to the present.

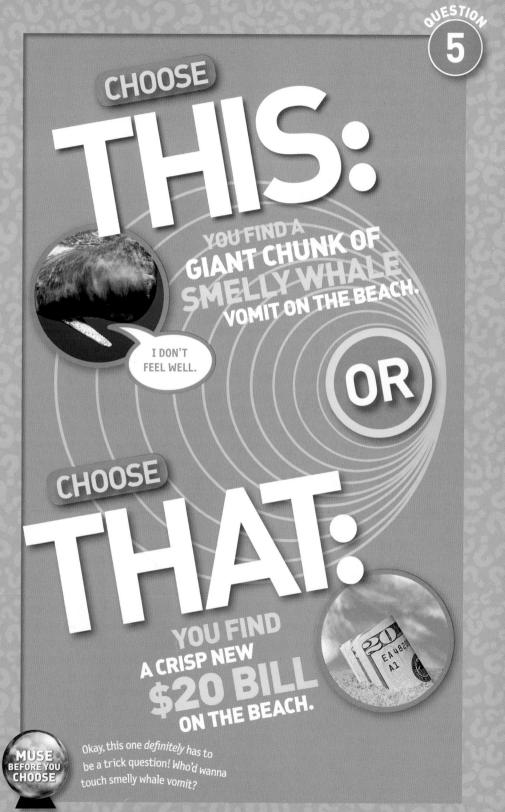

IF YOU CHOSE **THIS:**

Congrats, you're stinking rich! Whale vomit—otherwise known as **AMBERGRIS**—is a true treasure of the sea. This waxy substance builds in the bellies of sperm whales as a protective barrier around tough-to-stomach food items (such as the beaks of giant squid, the whales' favorite snack). Once upchucked into the ocean, ambergris bobs about for decades until it's nice and smelly. Ripe pieces are highly prized by the perfume industry, which pays a fortune for fragrant nuggets. A ten-year-old boy vacationing in Wales recently discovered a lump worth almost $6,000. That's what we call gross profit!

IF YOU CHOSE **THAT:**

Congrats on the extra spending money. Think of all the things you can do! Why not splurge on a movie? You would even have enough leftover cash to buy a small popcorn. Better yet, buy another copy of this book and share with a friend!

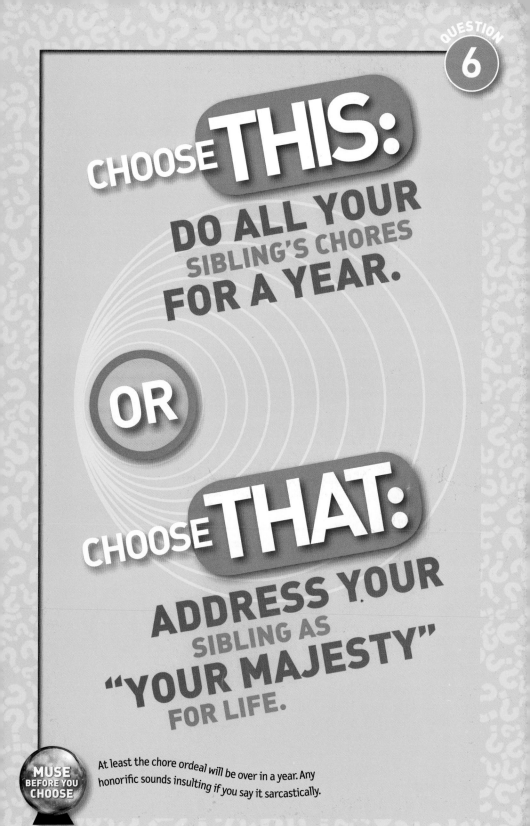

CHOOSE **THIS:**

DO ALL YOUR SIBLING'S CHORES FOR A YEAR.

OR

CHOOSE **THAT:**

ADDRESS YOUR SIBLING AS "YOUR MAJESTY" FOR LIFE.

MUSE BEFORE YOU CHOOSE

At least the chore ordeal will be over in a year. Any honorific sounds insulting if you say it sarcastically.

IF YOU CHOSE **THIS**:

Then look at the bright side of this unfortunate turn of events: Perhaps you can petition your parents to pay you your sibling's allowance, too. After all, you're the one rolling up your sleeves and doing **DOUBLE THE WORK.** Oh, and be glad you didn't have to assume your sibling's duties in the Middle Ages, when a typical kid was put to work gathering firewood, looking after the livestock, fetching buckets of water, and—if the kid was a knight's squire—scouring rust from armor using nothing but pee-soaked sand.

IF YOU CHOSE **THAT**:

Talk about a royal pain. Not even real-life siblings of kings and queens had to call their throne-warming kin "Your Majesty," an honorific reserved for **EUROPEAN MONARCHS** since the 16th century. (The family of King George VI of England nicknamed him "Bertie," short for his first name, Albert.) Sure, your brother and sister will get a kick out of the fancy title, but eventually the novelty will wear off. Shout enough "Your Majesties" across the dinner table or mall food court and eventually your red-faced sibling will beg you to go back to a first-name basis. In the meantime, things could be worse. At least your nickname isn't Bertie.

CHOOSE

THIS:

EVERYTHING YOU EAT TASTES LIKE HOT DOGS.

OR

CHOOSE

THAT:

YOU CAN'T MOVE UNLESS YOU'RE DANCING.

MUSE BEFORE YOU CHOOSE

Never complaining about eating your veggies. Getting strange looks for putting mustard on your ice cream. A trip to the fridge is exercise. Feeling awkward at funerals.

IF YOU CHOSE THIS:

Why not parlay your fervor for frankfurter flavor into a career in competitive eating? At the annual Nathan's Famous **HOT DOG EATING CONTEST,** the Super Bowl of eating contests, "gastro-athletes" have ten minutes to gobble up as many hot dogs as possible. They're allowed to snap the franks in half and soak the buns in water—which makes the doughy mess slide down easier. (Yum!) The world record is 69 hot dogs. Winning requires more than a hearty appetite, though. Gastro-athletes train their stomachs to stretch beyond doctor-approved limits, and even then many pro eaters still experience disqualifying "reversals" in the heat of competition. They don't just lose—they lose their lunch!

IF YOU CHOSE THAT:

Woo-hoo! Someone's ready for a 24-hour dance party! But before you limber up to boogie through life, you ought to know what you're *really* in for. After succumbing to sore feet, stomach problems, and sheer exhaustion, Indian dancer Kalamandalam Hemalatha landed in the hospital in 2010 following 63 hours of marathon **MOHINIYATTAM DANCING** (a classical Indian dance). But fear not: She got her groove back a few months later to set a Guinness World Record, dancing for 123 hours and 15 minutes with just a five-minute break each day. No wonder she's known as the "dancing queen of Kerala" (her home state in southern India).

CHOOSE **THIS:**

DRESS IN CLOTHING THAT'S TRANSPARENT.

OR

CHOOSE **THAT:**

DRESS IN CLOTHING MADE OF TOILET PAPER.

Do you sunburn easily? Strategically placing stains for privacy. Never needing to look for a tissue. Rain would really ruin your day.

MUSE
BEFORE YOU
CHOOSE

IF YOU CHOSE **THIS**:

Think people will chuckle at your transparent attire? Consider this: No one would dare laugh at the largest land carnivore, and it has see-through "clothes," too. The **POLAR BEAR** might look white and fluffy, but its fur isn't white at all. Each hair is actually translucent, with a hollow core that traps heat. The fur looks white only because of the way it reflects light (just like snowflakes look white even though they're transparent). If you were brave enough to brush aside a polar bear's dense coat, you'd see that its skin is actually as black as its nose!

IF YOU CHOSE **THAT**:

Don't pooh-pooh that TP T-shirt. It turns out **TOILET PAPER** can make a fashion statement in the hands of the right designer. One website in particular holds an annual contest for the best TP dress. Using glue, tape, thread, and lots of toilet paper as fabric (as many as 50 rolls of the plushy stuff), contestants create elaborate gowns complete with ruffles, embroidery, and lace. One winner two years running complemented her paper creation with a brooch, headpiece, and bracelet—all made of TP, of course.

Funny Duds...

If you think toilet paper is a funky fabric, imagine donning duds stitched together from sponges, balloons, money, or even meat. All of these materials have made their way down the fashion runway at one time or another, which just goes to show: Fashion can be freaky!

DID YOU **KEEP TRACK** OF EACH THIS AND THAT ?

TURN THE PAGE TO SEE WHAT YOUR CHOICES SAY ABOUT YOU!

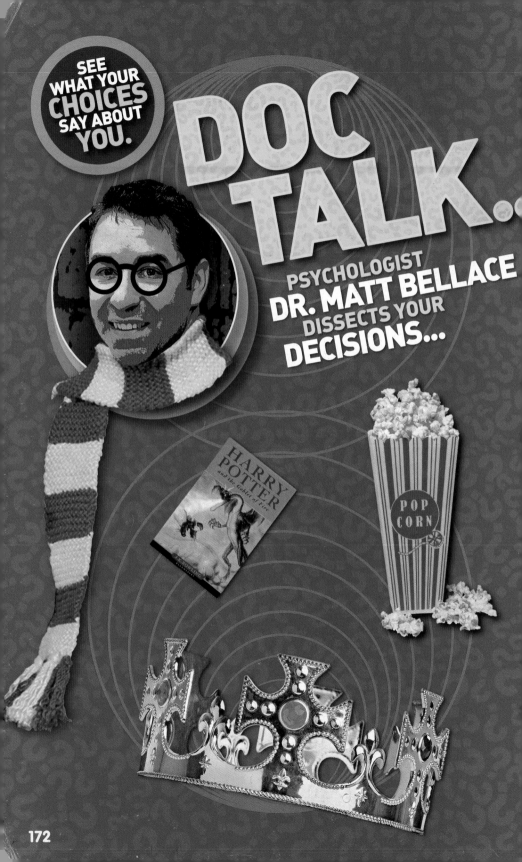

SEE WHAT YOUR CHOICES SAY ABOUT YOU.

DOC TALK...

PSYCHOLOGIST **DR. MATT BELLACE** DISSECTS YOUR **DECISIONS...**

ANALYZE
THIS!

CHOOSE THIS, If you mostly picked you should feel great knowing that you're able to make logical choices in absurd situations. After all, life will sometimes present you with no positive options. Your personality style doesn't shy away from tough choices but rather chooses the least unpleasant route for the long term. I can't imagine what sneezing and tasting hot dogs forever will be like, but at least you'll be done with your sibling's chores when a year is up!

ANALYZE
THAT!

CHOOSE THAT, If you mostly picked you're an impulsive decision-maker who doesn't always think through all of the consequences of your actions. When presented with two difficult choices, you might get distracted by what sounds like a good deal—only to find out it's the harder or less profitable road. Fear not! The decision-making part of the human brain doesn't fully develop until age 25, so you've got time to learn some lessons. One trick is to slow yourself down before reaching a decision. Even a 30-second break to mull over the options can give you time to make a better choice.

CREDITS

CREDITS

Published by the National Geographic Society
John M. Fahey, *Chairman of the Board and Chief Executive Officer*
Declan Moore, *Executive Vice President; President, Publishing and Travel*
Melina Gerosa Bellows, *Publisher; Chief Creative Officer, Books, Kids, and Family*

Prepared by the Book Division
Hector Sierra, *Senior Vice President and General Manager*
Nancy Laties Feresten, *Senior Vice President, Kids Publishing and Media*
Jennifer Emmett, *Vice President, Editorial Director, Kids Books*
Eva Absher-Schantz, *Design Director, Kids Publishing and Media*
Jay Sumner, *Director of Photography, Kids Publishing*
R. Gary Colbert, *Production Director*
Jennifer A. Thornton, *Director of Managing Editorial*

Staff for This Book
Becky Baines, *Project Editor*
David Seager, *Art Director*
Hillary Leo, *Associate Photo Editor*
Simon Renwick, *Designer*
Ariane Szu-Tu, *Editorial Assistant*
Callie Broaddus, *Design Production Assistant*
Margaret Leist, *Photo Assistant*
Grace Hill, *Associate Managing Editor*
Michael O'Connor, *Production Editor*
Lewis R. Bassford, *Production Manager*
Susan Borke, *Legal and Business Affairs*

Production Services
Phillip L. Schlosser, *Senior Vice President*
Chris Brown, *Vice President, NG Book Manufacturing*
George Bounelis, *Senior Production Manager*
Nicole Elliott, *Director of Production*
Rachel Faulise, *Manager*
Robert L. Barr, *Manager*